More praise for *Walking Together through Illness*

"Through their relationship with God through Jesus Christ, through sharing their stories with each other and with others, and through building relationship with others, [this husband and wife] discovered the capacity not only to meet difficulties head-on, but they also found the resources for thriving as individuals, as a couple, and as member of God's family. For those who are facing difficult life circumstances, this is a must read."

— Edward P. Wimberly, Vice President Academic Services/
  Provost, Interdenominational Theological Center

"The authors' helpful chronicle of [their] journey through the emotional ups and downs of coping with an unexpected chronic illness outlines twelve tasks crucial to the emotional, psychological, and spiritual health of patients and caregivers. The guidance they provide is both practical and inspiring, as they also recognize the importance of creating a relational climate conducive to the welcoming and support of friends, volunteers, and professionals who provide the necessary services upon which patients and their families depend."

—J. Jeffrey Means, Director of Professional Education,
  Des Moines Pastoral Counseling Center

WALKING TOGETHER THROUGH ILLNESS

TWELVE STEPS FOR CAREGIVERS AND CARE RECEIVERS

WANDA SCOTT BLEDSOE AND MILT BLEDSOE

MINNEAPOLIS

WALKING TOGETHER THROUGH ILLNESS
Twelve Steps for Caregivers and Care Receivers

Copyright © 2006 Wanda Scott and Milton Bledsoe. All rights reserved. Except for brief quotations in critical articles or reviews, no part of this book may be reproduced in any manner without prior written permission from the publisher. Visit www.augsburgfortress.org/copyrights/contact.asp or write to Permissions, Augsburg Fortress, Publishers, Box 1209, Minneapolis, MN 55440-1209.

Large-quantity purchases or custom editions of this book are available at a discount from the publisher. For more information, contact the sales department at Augsburg Fortress, Publishers, 1-800-328-4648, or write to: Sales Director, Augsburg Fortress, Publishers, Box 1209, Minneapolis, MN 55440-1209.

Library of Congress Cataloging-in-Publication Data
Bledsoe, Wanda Scott, 1945–
  Walking together through illness : twelve steps for caregivers and care receivers / by Wanda Scott Bledsoe and Milt Bledsoe.
     p. cm.
  Includes bibliographical references.
  ISBN-13: 978-0-8066-5292-4
  ISBN-10: 0-8066-5292-6 (pbk. : alk. paper)
  1. Caregiver—Religious life. 2. Sick—Religious life. 3. Consolation. I. Bledsoe, Milt, 1941– II. Title.
  BV4910.9.B54 2006
  259'.4—dc22   2006017652

Scripture passages are from the Holy Bible, New International Version, copyright © 1973, 1978, 1984 International Bible Society. Used by permission of Zondervan Publishing House. All rights reserved.

Cover design by Dave Meyer; Cover photo © Jack Hollingsworth/Photodisc Red/Getty Images. Used by permission.
Book design by Michelle L. N. Cook

The paper used in this publication meets the minimum requirements of American National Standard for Information Sciences—Permanence of Paper for Printed Library Materials, ANSI Z329.48-1984.

Manufactured in the U.S.A.

10   09   08   07   06   1   2   3   4   5   6   7   8   9   10

On to Others Care

When daily life grows harsh,
By blows destructive, age or war,
It reaches out for you to care—
Like Jesus at your door.
I ask of Him,
What can I do?
The suffering seems more.
I cannot fall.
He grabs my hand
And lifts my spirit poor!

When weary days close in
With longing for life before
He gives the gift of others
To ease the present chore.
I call on Him,
Where will this lead?
The stress I feel four-score!
He answers,
"On to others care"
Will lift your spirit poor!

—Robert Lee Larson
A gift for our good friends, Milt and Wanda

Contents

Foreword

Contemporary medical practice is rapidly becoming impersonal. Today's physicians frequently are pressured to see more patients in their daily schedule, leaving little time for interactions with their patients beyond the chief complaint of the appointment. Too often the psychological, social, and quality of life concerns of the patient who has a chronic illness are not discussed. If the patient does mention feelings and concerns, these issues are addressed usually after the more concrete physical symptoms and signs of the disease. Spiritual issues generally have little impact on the medical interview.

Wanda and Milton have shared their journey through illness with me during our visits in my office over the last several years. However, I confess that, although I am their family physician, many of the details presented in this book were new to me. Based upon past medical, surgical, and social history, we think that we know our patients well, yet this knowledge really is only a small facet of their lives.

Upon reviewing the book, I was amazed at Wanda and Milton's open and honest dialog regarding what is the ultimate test of faith, love, and marriage: chronic illness coupled with severe debility and pain. Milton's rapid regression from vitality and independence to becoming wheelchair-bound only complicates the issue. Their story is indeed compelling and courageous.

This book is well suited to the non-clinical examination of the stepwise process that most patients and their families endure with chronic illness, yet the style of hearing both sides of the journey is novel. Coping with illness, pain, loneliness, self-doubt, and uncertainty regarding recovery are undoubtedly on the minds of both caregiver and care receiver, although clear expression of these concerns may not be well communicated between them. Wanda and Milton have done a wonderful job of bringing the reader into their personal world, to meet their fears, challenges, victories, and setbacks in a way that few of us could find the courage to explore for ourselves, much less in a public display such as this book. My adoration of their faith and health journey is obvious, but truly the greatest good for this effort is when others in a similar situation avoid problems and grow stronger, based on the recommendations and scripture passages contained herein. I hope doctors and patients, healthcare workers, pastors, and future caregivers can all benefit from the loving experiences that are so openly presented here. It has been my honor to know and care for Milton and Wanda, and they are truly a blessing to their families and friends. I hope that you feel the same as I did upon finishing this book.

—Dr. Kelly McKerahan

Preface

Dear Readers,

My husband and co-author, Milt, and I are delighted you have chosen to share our journey of faith written from Milt's perspective as care receiver and mine as caregiver. We are grateful for this opportunity because writing this book has enabled us to talk with each other in ways we haven't communicated previously, and it has allowed us to see that we have missed so much. We hope that our story will inspire and motivate you to begin walking *and* talking together through the illness that brings you together as caregiver and care receiver. It is our prayer that, in doing so, you will experience your own faith journey with new insights, new hope, new ideas, and new reasons to celebrate God in your everyday lives.

We encourage you to do the journaling activity at the end of each section and thereby create a priceless written account of your own faith journey that you can treasure and share with others. We have also set up a Web site, www.hisrosesandthorns.com, to keep you apprised of Milton's progress and the on-going path of our journey. Finally, if you know caregivers and care receivers who might benefit from this book, please give them a copy to support them in their journey.

"May the grace of the Lord Jesus Christ, and the love of God, and the fellowship of the Holy Spirit be with you all" (2 Corinthians 13:14).

Wanda Scott Bledsoe

—Wanda Scott Bledsoe, Caregiver

Dear Readers,

This book and my contribution to it are Wanda's idea. She is truly a remarkable person. I met Wanda in September 1962 at a fraternity party at the University of Kansas. We didn't speak on that occasion, but I noticed Wanda's special quality at that time. Our first conversation took place in September 1964 after the morning worship service at First Baptist Church in Kansas City, Kansas. Much had happened during the previous two years that made me appear to be a different person in Wanda's eyes. The next Saturday night we had our first date. Two years later we were married. Wanda and I are now in the fortieth year of our journey together. Although neither of us ever imagined the path this journey would take, we know God continues to bless us. Wanda has been a devoted caregiver for me in the same manner that our mothers cared for their husbands. I count my blessings each day that Wanda is able to remain emotionally and physically healthy. While Wanda thought the message of this book would be how well the care receiver does when he or she has a devoted caregiver, our physician said, "No, the true, exciting message is how the caregiver—in this case, Wanda—flourishes instead of breaking down under this tremendous load."

How does Wanda take such good care of me? How does she create and maintain an inviting home and make sure I am surrounded with loving and caring people, while still looking like the beautiful bride I married almost forty years ago? How does she continue her commitment to women's ministry and her work as an author and inspirational speaker? I think the answer is in the story that you are about to read. I was blessed to marry an angel and I give thanks to God each day for my wife, Wanda.

"Do not be anxious about anything, but in everything, by prayer and petition, with thanksgiving, present your requests to God. And the peace of God, which transcends all understanding, will guard your hearts and your minds in Christ Jesus" (Philippians 4:6 7).

—Milt Bledsoe, Care Receiver

A Tribute to Two Wonderful Caregivers

Wanda's Mother—Ruby Dulan Scott

I smile when I see books titled, *All I Need to Know I Learned . . . ,* because they remind me of my dear mother. Truly, all I need to know I learned from my mother who devoted her life to seeing that my sister, Pat, and I received a solid Christian upbringing. My mother and my deceased father, Clovis Scott, were wonderful role models who took us to Sunday school and worship, and who worked diligently in our church. They also modeled the Christian life by helping others. At the age of ninety-one, my mother continues to visit those who are sick and homebound as well as teach an adult Sunday school class.

My mother also modeled for me the role of loving caregiver. My father died in 1994 after a ten-year battle with Alzheimer's disease. When my father's condition deteriorated to the point where he couldn't care for himself, my mother cared for him. I remember visiting my parents and telling mom that I would help Daddy with his personal care so she could sit and relax. While I struggled to shave my father, clean his dentures, convince him to sit in the bathtub, and get him dressed, I wondered, "How does she do all this, plus keep house, prepare meals, take Daddy to doctor's appointments, and still have energy to travel by plane to visit us once or twice each year?"

My mother's answer was, "First, trust God for the strength you need. Stay in God's word to receive the encouragement, comfort, guidance, love, and, yes, conviction we need to make sure we are on the right track." She also told me she had to move quickly to get everything done!

How I admire my mother. I am grateful that when Milton first became ill I knew how to "move" and lovingly care for him as I had seen my mother "move" and lovingly care for my father. I am also grateful that I already had a strong relationship with God, thanks to my parents having raised me in the faith.

Milt's Mother—Dorothy Spencer Bledsoe

My mother was a schoolteacher in the Kansas City, Kansas, school district until she married my father in 1926 and had to resign because there was a law at that time prohibiting married women from teaching in public schools. However, she continued to teach Sunday school at First Baptist Church until her health failed in 1977. My mother had a profound influence upon my life as a Christian, making sure that my sisters and I went to Sunday school and church every Sunday morning, often attending evening services as well.

I observed my mother in her role as a caregiver on many occasions, and she always modeled what it means to "love thy neighbor." She cared with ceaseless devotion for my Aunt Elizabeth even as advanced Alzheimer's made my aunt more and more difficult to manage. She also prepared meals for our neighbors who were older and in poor health and helped them with household chores. Her service was given freely to the glory of God and out of great gratitude and love for her neighbors. When my father, who was diabetic and suffered from glaucoma, was declared legally blind, my mother assisted him with daily needs so he could continue to write articles for local newspapers.

Despite her busy schedule, my mother took a job at the Kansas State School for the Blind and worked there for more than ten years. I remember visiting the school for my mother's retirement party, and, realizing that everybody loved my mother, I thought I would never again see someone care so tirelessly and selflessly for others. But guess what? As I continue to recuperate, I see more of my mother in Wanda, my wife and caregiver, with every passing day.

Twelve Steps to Get the Most Out of This Book

1. Thoughtfully consider each of the twelve steps.

2. Discuss how you might benefit from the caregiver and care receiver tips.

3. Talk with each other about how each step applies to your particular situation.

4. Do the journaling activities and share your entries with each other, as you feel comfortable.

5. Revisit steps as needed.

6. Enjoy each other, and keep talking together.

7. Consider what you would like to do with your journals when they are complete.

8. Contact the caring family and friends you name in your journals and say thanks.

9. Ask those closest to you what they think you should do with your journals.

10. Consider who might benefit from hearing your story. How might you share it?

11. Experience the joy of helping others even as you reach out to others for the help you need.

12. Pray often, and don't forget to count your blessings.

Step One

Tell Your Story

"The Lord is good, a refuge in times of trouble.

He cares for those who trust in him" (Nahum 1:7).

Milt's Story

Praise be to our Lord and Savior, Jesus Christ. Amen! Wanda asked that I begin my story with my trip to Tijuana, Mexico, a few years ago. But the story really began in Seattle, Washington, more than 20 years ago, when I met Connie Jacobsen. Connie had been the director of Young Life, a Christian-based organization that helps young people come to know Jesus Christ. Later he founded a ministry called Telios to help men come to know and love Jesus, as well. Connie often called me at work to invite me to lunch. I never had time, but he was both patient and persistent. We finally met for lunch and that was the beginning of a special relationship that has lasted all these years.

It wasn't long after my lunch with Connie that I got a call from the chairperson of the Young Life committee in the central area of Seattle asking if Wanda and I would consider joining the committee. After prayerful consideration, and with Connie's encouragement, we decided to do so. Within a couple of years, a new executive director was hired and I became the committee chairperson. One of my first projects as chairperson was to help plan a banquet to raise money for new director's vision for the Young Life committee. Committee members suggested several people to be the keynote speaker for the banquet, but everyone spoke highly of Tom Skinner, so we contacted him and he accepted.

I didn't know about Tom before hearing him speak the night of the banquet, but his speech about character development and how best to measure character made a definite impact on my life. Tom truly was all that had been promised and more. I had the privilege to spend two evenings with him when he came to speak, and I was moved by both his message and his life.

Tom grew up in Harlem, the son of a preacher who led a double life as a gang member. Eventually he became a preacher himself but with a very non-traditional ministry. In addition to leading crusades in inner-city communities during the civil rights movement, Tom wrote four books and was much sought after as a public speaker. I listened closely to his profound assessment that the entries in our checkbooks and date books show how we spend our time and money. In other words, they reveal what we value most and provide a fairly accurate indication of our true character. Over dinner the next evening, we committee members learned more about Tom and his ministry in Newark, New Jersey. Those two evenings with Tom turned out to be pivotal as I continued my walk with Christ.

Feet on fire, the beginning

Wanda and I moved to Southern California thirteen years ago. Before leaving Seattle, I enjoyed one last lunch with a special group of men who had been my faith partners. They asked me what my ministry was going to be in Temecula, California. I told them I didn't know what God had in store for me, but that I knew God had a plan. Then we prayed together that I would continue to be in fellowship with other men.

We joined Hope Lutheran Church in Temecula, California. Since there were no small groups for men, I decided to start a

Monday Night Football Bible study group. We met in our home, and the men took turns providing dinner, which we ate while we watched the first half of the game. Then we turned off the television and spent halftime studying God's word. For the first two years, we only met during football season, and we always watched the second half of the game. After that, we began to meet year round, and during football season, we'd spend the entire second half in Bible study.

I continued to keep in touch with Connie and to share my new ministry with him. When our church held its first men's advance a few years later, I invited Connie to facilitate our inaugural gathering. It was at this time that Connie told me that a group from the Pacific Northwest planned to travel to Tijuana, Mexico, to build homes for disenfranchised people. We shared visions of making this a joint venture of men from Washington and California, but it was several years before we could coordinate our schedules. In October 2002, it looked like our vision would become a reality, but in the end only one Californian (me) and nineteen guys from Seattle, including Connie, made the trip. Still, what we lacked in numbers, we more than made up in enthusiasm, so we decided to go ahead with the original plan to build two houses in four days.

We traveled to the job site in two white vans on unpaved streets through squalor that I hadn't seen since visiting my mother's home in Carrollton, Missouri, as a child. But whereas in Missouri the signs of despair and poverty had gone on for only a few blocks, in Mexico they lasted for miles. It was hard to hold back tears as people stopped to watch our caravan pass. Only later did I learn that they looked upon us as a promise that God had not forgotten them, and soon some of their neighbors would have new homes.

The first thing you must do when building a house is set the foundation. In our case, this meant laying out a concrete slab. Since we had neither a cement truck nor a cement mixer, this work had to be done by hand. We formed a cone of sand, rock, and concrete. Then we dug out the top of the cone and slowly poured water into the hollowed out depression. As the water seeped through, we pushed out the wet cement. We labored in 100 degree heat, making slow progress on the hardest work I had ever done in my life. By mid-afternoon, the slab was complete. As we waited for the cement to dry, we learned that the home we were building would be for a family with three children. The father was a cabdriver who worked at night while the rest of the family slept in a lean-to erected on the back end of their property, which they had purchased a year earlier for $10,000. For a full year they had prayed that someday God would send someone to build their new home. Thank God that day had finally come.

Even though I had no expertise as a cook, I had been assigned to head up the kitchen operation, with rotating teams of men to help me prepare the evening meal. This meant that I had to return to the base camp earlier than the rest of the crew. When I arrived at camp after that first day on the job, I noticed that my feet were sore and burning. I took a quick shower, thinking I would get some relief. It didn't help, but since I had a meal to prepare, I tried to ignore my discomfort.

Mealtimes offered opportunity for us to develop a special bond with each other by sharing the personal stories of our journeys with Christ. I enjoyed hearing the stories that evening, in spite of the fact that my feet felt like they were on fire. Since things always seem better in the morning, I went to bed anticipating that a good night's sleep would bring me relief. I awoke in the middle of the night needing to go to the restroom, and discovered that I could not get up from the floor. Fortunately I had put my air mattress under a window so I pulled myself to my feet by hanging onto the windowsill. After considerable struggle, I eventually made it outside and across the parking lot to the bathroom facility. But for the next three nights, I slept in the front passenger seat of one of the vans, rather than on my air mattress on the floor of an orphanage storeroom with the rest of the crew

My first day on the job, I easily had hoisted fifty-pound bags of cement over my head and bounded up and down stairs improvised from old tires filled with sand. By day two I had gone from feeling like an energetic eighteen year-old to acting like a feeble eighty-one year-old. My feet were still on fire and I couldn't get oriented. I even needed help getting up and down the stairs. While two other men had been too ill to come to the job site, I struggled through the day, working fifteen minutes followed by five minutes of rest. It was even hotter than the day before, and I got weaker by the moment. I was glad when I got to leave early to prepare the evening meal.

In preparation for the trip, I had bought a twenty-four-ounce hammer to use for framing houses. But in my weakened state, I could barely lift it. After considerable effort, I managed to drive in a nail, only to discover that it was a few inches from the correct spot. Then Connie and I, the oldest crew members, were put to work painting the plywood siding for the house. I could roll only a couple of the strokes before I would have to rest on the back of the van that was parked nearby. Still, slowly but surely, Connie and I got the siding painted.

On the morning of the third day, I was asked to sweep out the two rooms of our newly constructed house. As I labored to complete this simple task, it became even more apparent that something was terribly wrong with me. There were very few items that I was able to move without assistance. As I struggled with the task at hand, I sensed a cooling breeze within the room, which was strange since the only windows in the house were on the opposite side of the wind's direction. Nevertheless, I was grateful for the relief, and I began to think back to my first job when I was thirteen years old and my neighbor and good friend John "Butch" Sams taught me how to sweep. I felt his presence in a very special way while I swept that day, so when I was called on to share my faith story after the noon meal, I told the men about Butch.

Butch was a big kid, two years older than I, who had a reputation in our neighborhood for being a bully. He attended the Methodist church, and I was a Baptist. I was an honor student. Even though he was older, Butch had been held back a year because of poor grades, so we graduated from high school together. In his own way, Butch looked out for me, and he always let me know when he was going to leave a job so I could apply to replace him. Then he would stay long enough to orient me. Thanks to Butch's help, I learned a lot and earned some much needed money.

After graduation, Butch and I lost touch, until four years later when he came to Kansas University for the Kansas Relays. I was glad to see him and to learn that he had given his life to Christ and was now teaching Sunday school at the Methodist church. He also announced that he had a wonderful job, a new car, and he was engaged to be married.

I sincerely was happy for Butch, but I couldn't help thinking just how much our fortunes had changed since graduation. His was a success story. On the other hand, because of financial difficulties, I had been forced to drop out of school. In order to have enough to return to the University of Kansas the next semester, I was driving a cab and attending a computer programming school at the time. I ran into Butch later that same night and offered him a bed at the fraternity house since it was so late. He thanked me for the offer but told me he had to get back to Kansas City in time to co-teach his Sunday school class with his fiancée the next morning. I said good-bye to Butch but continued to think about him for the rest of the weekend.

The following Monday morning as I walked up the hill to my yellow cab job, I met our neighbor, Mrs. Browne, and learned from her the shocking news that Butch had been killed in a car accident. I didn't believe what I was hearing until I read the story myself on the front page of the morning newspaper. My envy of Butch's success gave way to my anger at God for Butch's senseless death.

I was so conflicted and bitter that I doubted I would even attend Butch's funeral. But encouraged by both my mother and a classmate, I finally decided to go. During the service, I found out what remarkable things Butch had accomplished in the four years since high school graduation. I saw his beautiful fiancée, and I heard Butch eulogized as a great leader and beloved teacher. The minister assured us that Butch was now at peace with his heavenly father and had heard the words, "well done thou good and faithful servant." He went on to say that the message for the day wasn't for Butch but for young people like me who were struggling to find their purpose and seeking their way to be about their heavenly father's business. The message was hard but true. Without Butch's on-the-job training, I had lost my way.

Not long after Butch's funeral, I was overcome with a sense a guilt and a severe case of the "what ifs." What if I had insisted he stay overnight with me rather than drive back to Kansas City? My depression continued for several weeks, but my faith walk became stronger and my life had a renewed sense of purpose.

When I finished telling my story, my new band of brothers from the Pacific Northwest expressed their support for me with words, hugs, and prayers. It was amazing how close we had become to one another in the span of four days, and we had managed to build a couple houses, too. Although I was suffering unbearable pain, I was also filled with anticipation of returning soon to build more homes with these brothers in Christ. That was my vision, but things don't always go as we plan.

Back in Temecula, I shared the story of my incredible Mexico experience with Wanda and with our church congregation during worship services the following Sunday. But I didn't say much about the pain in my feet, which continued to ebb and flow, with nights being the worst. Because I now had difficulty walking even short distances without needing to sit down or lean on something, I changed my daily routine so I didn't need to do much walking. I also gave up the three-mile power walk that normally began my day as well as the exercise plan I had designed to help me lose weight and control my diabetes.

In December, two months after my return from Mexico, I had to make an unscheduled trip to Orlando to host a reception and make a presentation. This was my first flight since Mexico, and even the walk from my car to the airport was a struggle. When I deplaned in Orlando, I asked an airport employee for directions to the hotel where I was staying. To my relief, she pointed toward an escalator just four steps from where I was standing. God was smiling on me that day, because as weak as I was, I couldn't have walked much further.

Wanda and I spent Christmas in Seattle with our daughter, Shelly, her husband, Ken, and our grandson, Conner. Conner was sick during our visit and by the time we got home, Wanda wasn't feeling well either. Although I usually am immune to such maladies, I also came down with the bug and it lingered with me for more than a month.

I was scheduled to return to Seattle for an important business meeting in mid-February. I felt terrible and was dreading another flight. At a friend's encouragement, I went to urgent care to get a doctor's clearance to fly. He prescribed antibiotics for an upper respiratory infection and drops for an ear infection that had also developed.

The fall that saved my life

I had a busy agenda in Seattle, and without a rental car, I had to traverse the hills of downtown Seattle on foot. The shortness of breath caused by the upper respiratory infection coupled with the pain in my ears only added to my struggle to walk even short distances. I ended up skipping one reception and was late for dinner with my son-in-law and grandson. That night I didn't sleep at all and I would not have made it to my business event if the bank hadn't provided a shuttle from my hotel to the convention center. Such service hadn't been provided in previous years so this truly was an unexpected but much appreciated blessing.

When we arrived at the convention center, I missed a step and almost fell getting off the shuttle. Once inside, I looked for somewhere to sit down but there wasn't any kind of seating in the lobby. After waiting nearly twenty minutes, we were allowed to enter the auditorium. I had a difficult time getting oriented in the dim light, as I carefully made my way to my seat in one of the upper decks. Although I had no history of being claustrophobic, I felt very confined and uncomfortable as we waited for the program to begin. Amplified music blaring through the auditorium sound system and the shouting and clapping of my colleagues added to my misery and disorientation. When the event finally began, I had so much difficulty getting focused that I decided to leave. I managed to make it to an exit and headed to the lobby, hoping to find something to drink. I desperately needed something to give me a little energy.

After a few minutes in the quiet lobby I felt a little less disoriented and was about to return to the auditorium when I spotted my boss arriving for the meeting. I told him that I was not feeling well and he offered to give me a ride back to the hotel where I could rest. I gratefully accepted his offer and waited in the lobby while he brought the car around. By the time he arrived I could hardly stand, and when I tried to take a step, I fell and cut my head on a planter. Blood gushed from my wound, but I remained conscious. I remember my boss, aided by a kindly stranger, helping me to my feet and getting me into the car. We rushed to a hospital emergency room where the hospital staff checked my vitals and made some astonishing discoveries.

The attending physician told me that I was in serious shape. My blood sugar was elevated and I was severely dehydrated. Basically my body was in "starvation mode" and I needed to be hospitalized for treatment and observation. The emergency room personnel started me on an insulin drip and stitched up my head wound.

All this time my boss had been trying to reach Wanda, but she was not at home. He tried her cell phone and got her voice mail but decided it would be less traumatic if he spoke to her directly. They finally connected, and after giving her information about my condition, he told her to make arrangements to come to Seattle as soon as possible

It was about 9:00 P.M. when Wanda and our daughter, Shelly, arrived at the hospital. By that time, I was out of immediate danger, due to the alert work of the medical team and the fact that I was blessed to be in one of the best hospitals in the country. I remained in Virginia Mason Medical Center for four days while the bank arranged for Wanda and me to fly first-class back to California on Saturday.

I returned to work in my office on the following Monday but agreed that I would restrict my traveling until I was back in good health. The pain in my feet continued unabated, and I decided to consult with a podiatrist. Without doing an examination or even observing my painful walk, he told me I could resume exercising but that I should buy new running shoes every six weeks. I followed his advice and bought new running shoes, but I only used them once. My first power walk ended about a block from our house when excruciating pain in my feet left me leaning against a retaining wall for several minutes before I could limp slowly and gingerly home. That evening the pain in my feet moved up my legs, and finally I shared with Wanda all that I had been going through.

Jury duty

Earlier in the year, I had been summoned for jury duty but had been excused from serving because of a business obligation. While recuperating from my hospitalization, I received a second summons telling me to report for duty on May 15 to U.S. District Court in Riverside, about forty-five miles from our home.

Since I was one of a hundred citizens from whom twelve jurors and three alternates would be chosen, I figured my odds of being excused were very good. In fact, I already had planned to use the week as vacation time. Before noon, twenty-four potential jurors had been selected, and my name was the first on the list. Following questions and challenges by lawyers for both the plaintiff and the defendant, the judge announced that a final jury had been selected. Milt Bledsoe was now Juror Number 1.

The plaintiff in the case alleged that while in police detention he had received injuries that caused nerve damage to his arms. Over the next eight days, I heard expert testimony from neurologists, pain managers, podiatrists, and others in related fields. Since it was obvious that the plaintiff was suffering pain much like what I was experiencing in my feet and legs, I paid rapt attention to all of the testimony and took copious notes. As the trial progressed, I put together a tentative game plan and a "dream team" to consult with about my own condition after the trial was over. It was a good thing that I was paying close attention because when deliberations ended, our trial notes became the property of the court.

I didn't waste any time after the trial ended before putting my plan in action. Wanda made an appointment with our family doctor who referred me to both a neurologist and a podiatrist. Within a week, I had been given a thorough examination by the podiatrist who suspected from my limp that my left leg had suffered nerve damage. My neurologist saw me a week later and immediately ordered a CT scan to determine whether or not I had had a stroke. Test results indicated that I hadn't suffered a stroke, but that I did have a pea-sized tumor at the base of my pituitary gland. After consulting with a neurosurgeon and undergoing yet another CT scan, we determined that it was best not to take any action on the tumor unless it grew larger. In the meantime, I would begin physical therapy to strengthen my left leg.

Driving with hand controls

Physical therapy (PT) started in early June, and by July 4, I had regressed from walking with a limp to using a cane and then a walker. The more I exercised, the weaker I got. This was baffling to the therapist and to me, so he referred me back to my neurologist and we agreed to stop the PT sessions.

During PT, my therapist had suggested that I consider having hand controls installed in our car to make it easier and safer for me to drive. Wanda and I talked it over and decided to install them in her SUV. On Thursday, we traveled to San Diego to have the SUV retrofitted. Early Saturday morning, I went out for my first solo drive with the new controls. After two hours, I felt quite relaxed.

I drove home, thinking about this new chapter in my life. All went very well until I got home. As I negotiated the slight incline of our driveway, the car began to stall. I knew instinctively to give it some gas, but instead of using the hand controls, as I had practiced all morning, I reverted to a fifty-year habit and stepped down on the accelerator. The car sped into the garage, through the back wall, and on into the guest bath. Before the dust had settled, I put the car in reverse and lurched out of the garage, back down the driveway, across the street and into our neighbor's garage. Since my foot was on both the brake and the accelerator, I left a trail of burned rubber the entire way. When the car came to a stop, I was showered with glass from the shattered windshield and water from our neighbor's ruptured irrigation system. The SUV was determined later to be a total loss, but no one, including me, was injured. What a blessing!

In spite of the accident, we kept that week's appointment with the neurologist. As I was too weak to stand or walk, Wanda wheeled me in using our newly acquired wheel chair. After reviewing my chart and the latest test results, the neurologist was convinced of his diagnosis. It turns out that I have a rare nerve disorder called Chronic Inflammatory Demyelinating Polyneuropathy (CIDP), a condition similar to Guillain-Barre Syndrome. Treatment would involve hospitalization and would include intravenous immunoglobulin (IVIg) therapy. I checked into the hospital that same day without ever returning home. Five days later, my neurologist discharged me after making arrangements for a nurse to come to our home twice a week to continue to administer the nerve rejuvenating IVIg. My neurologist's personal attention to my care, as well as the genuine warmth and interest of his office staff, endeared them to us from day one. Since my case was so severe, my neurologist initiated second opinions from among neurologists in the surrounding area. After more evaluations and tests, Wanda and I were more convinced than ever that my best chance for recovery rested in the hands of the neurologist. Later, we would consider our choice of doctor as one of the defining moments in our quest for an effective treatment plan.

This was a critical time for me. I can't stress enough how settled Wanda and I felt once we knew what I had and what my treatment would involve. My sense of relief was accompanied by an eagerness to pursue my goal to walk again. And so began a journey of challenges the likes of which I had never before experienced.

Wanda's Story

I watched in fascination as the pile of camping gear accumulated on the floor of our family room, all the while wondering why my husband, a banker who went off to work every day dressed in a suit and tie, would need a huge hammer and steel-toed work boots. I soon discovered that Milton was preparing for a weekend trip to Tijuana, Mexico, with a group of Christian men to help build houses for two families. "What a great way for these men to bond," I thought.

A changed man

I sensed immediately that there was something different about my husband when he returned from Tijuana on Sunday night. I listened in awe as he recounted the experience that had had such a profound impact on him. Little did we know at the time just how profound. Milton talked about the wonderful family who had scrimped and saved in the hope of one day owning a home of their own. He spoke of the family's excitement at having a home with solid walls rather than spaces divided off by blankets. I learned that the father drove a cab at night while his wife and three children slept on the couch. In the morning, the family moved outside to cook while the father slept on the couch. Tears came to my husband's eyes as he told of the love that he and others felt from this family.

Milton explained how he helped mix cement by hand, and then his voice softened as he told me of almost immediately feeling a burning sensation in his feet. He admitted that the pain had been almost excruciating, forcing him to spend the rest of the weekend sitting or lying on his inflatable bed; needing assistance to stand. On the last day, he told of feeling somewhat stronger and asking to be allowed to sweep up the debris that had accumulated on the cement floor. Even though it lacked heat and running water, the new two-room house was everything the family had hoped for. Everyone was proud of this home, and Milton wanted to have played a part.

Milton related that he had prayed to God for the strength to complete this small task, and that help had come in a very unusual way. Growing up, Milton had had a friend named Butch whom he had seen last on the day Butch died in a tragic car accident while Milton was in college. But forty years later, on a hot day in Mexico, Milton had sensed Butch's presence: "You can do it, Bled." My husband told me, "It was so real, Wanda. I will never forget my friend, Butch, staying with me until that floor was swept completely clean."

"What a wonderful story!" I replied through my own tears. "Where are you going to share it?"

"Oh, I'll just share it with the men tomorrow night," he replied. For several years Milton had opened our house to what is lovingly and laughingly referred to as "The Men's Monday Night Football Bible Study."

"Hmm," I responded. "I think more people than eight to ten guys need to hear this story. I'm speaking next Sunday; how about if you and I both bring the message?"

Milton was enthusiastic about the idea and our tag team delivery was well received. But after a couple of weeks, I began to forget Milton's incredible story.

Signs of trouble

Milton and I have struggled with our weight throughout our marriage, so when he began to lose weight that fall, I was pleased for him but also a bit envious. Weeks passed, and he continued to lose. One day I looked at him and thought, "He doesn't look healthy. In fact, he looks sick." But when I voiced my concern about his health, Milton assured me that he felt great and wanted to lose another forty pounds. When I look back at a photo taken of him that Christmas, I can't help but wish I had known just how sick my husband of nearly forty years really was.

In February, Milton was scheduled to attend the State of the Group address of the financial organization where he worked, but he had contracted a really nasty cold over Christmas. After consulting with a physician, Milton did fly to Seattle for the conference, but on the second day he felt so ill that he decided to skip his next meeting and return to his room to rest. As he stood to leave, he tripped over a planter, falling face forward and cutting his forehead in the process. Embarrassed, he claimed he was fine even as blood streamed down his face. Milton's boss, Lawrence, insisted that he take him to the emergency room—an act that saved Milton's life. Lawrence didn't know that Milton suffered from diabetes, and he was unaware that Milton had been finding it increasingly difficult since his trip to Mexico to control his blood sugar.

The emergency room staff worked feverishly to lower Milt's elevated heart rate and his blood sugar, which had skyrocketed from its normal 80s to a staggering 400 plus. When Milton was stable, Lawrence called me in Southern California where we reside and made arrangements to fly me to the hospital in Seattle where Milt had been admitted. My mind was in a fog as I fervently prayed for my husband's recovery.

Nurses taught my husband how to inject himself with insulin, and in a few days we were on our way back home. Even though I have a degree in nursing, Milton never asked for help with administering his insulin. I find this remarkable since Milton had always been squeamish around needles. The next few months were spent monitoring his blood sugar and trying out a new diet designed to help reverse diabetes. Our commitment to that diet brought Milton's blood sugar under control so that he no longer needed to inject himself with insulin. "We're home free," I thought as I joyously praised God.

The journey begins

Just when I relaxed, thinking our lives were getting back to normal, I noticed that Milton was limping. The days blurred as I watched the daily decline in my husband's ability to walk. One day he came home from work with a cane, and I became accustomed to knowing he was nearby by the click, click sound of the cane. Before long, however, Milton exchanged the cane for a walker with a seat that allowed him to turn around and sit down when he grew tired, as he did more and more frequently.

We were going from doctor to doctor seeking a diagnosis for the condition that was making Milton weaker by the day, so when he received a jury summons, I assumed he would ask to be excused. "You can't possibly serve on a jury in your condition," I exclaimed.

"It's my duty," he softly replied. And so each day Milton made the hour drive to the Riverside County Courthouse for jury duty.

A few days into the trial, Milton came home all excited. "Wanda, you won't believe how God is taking care of me," he said, his eyes shining brightly. "I understand now why I am on this jury." Milton went on to tell me that the plaintiff in the case claimed that arresting officers had handcuffed him so tightly that he had suffered permanent nerve damage in his hands and arms. Over the last few days, the jury had heard expert testimony pertinent to the case from several neurologists. As soon as the trial ended, Milton made an appointment with a neurologist, confident that this doctor would diagnose his condition so treatment could begin. Surely soon everything would be back to normal.

I remember one day as summer approached, I looked out the dining room window, and not knowing what was wrong with Milton, I thought, "Lord, we have both grown up in the faith. I guess we are going to get a chance to find out just how strong in the faith we really are. I hope we don't disappoint you." There was no answer. I turned from the window to help Milton with a task he could no longer perform without assistance . . . and so the journey began.

What were they thinking?

Milton's ability to walk continued to deteriorate. When he could no longer navigate without a wheelchair, I began accompanying him to doctor appointments. As I struggled to maneuver Milton's wheelchair around hairpin curves and through doors that did not open automatically, I complained more than once about facilities that weren't in compliance with standards established by the American Disabilities Act passed years earlier. I had been a medical center administrator at the time so I knew the law well. The struggles didn't end once we got into the facility. The next challenge involved getting Milton onto the examination table. I couldn't do it by myself, so I had to find someone to help me. One time a petite female medical assistant was called into service. Other times I depended on anyone standing in the hallway who responded to my call, "Will someone please come give us a hand?" We sincerely are thankful to all who graciously helped us with a task that clearly wasn't in their job description.

Giving up the car keys

Milton and I were invited to celebrate the Fourth of July at the home of good friends. We had a lovely time, and as we left, we thanked our friends profusely for inviting us. But while they walked with us to our car, Milton faltered and would have fallen if Mike had not been on one side and I on the other. "Why don't you let Wanda drive home?" Mike asked, his apprehension clearly evident in his voice.

Milt's response was an emphatic, "No, I'll be fine."

I spent the trip praying for God's safe deliverance, and spent a few more minutes upon our arrival giving thanks for God's care. Then I called my daughter and my mother to seek support for what I needed to do next.

They both agreed that Milton shouldn't be driving and that I needed to convince him to give up his car keys, at least for the time being. Hope reigned eternal that one day soon we would find out what was causing Milton's paralysis, and that a cure would be found. I knew my mother and daughter were right, but I also knew that this task would be easier said than done. I remembered how challenging it had been for friends to convince their elderly parents to relinquish their keys. The struggle, after all, really wasn't about giving up the keys to the car. The struggle was about relinquishing independence. Driving was important to me. If I were forced to give up my keys it would mean that a significant part of my life was over. The change would be even more significant for Milton because he always had been the breadwinner and head of our household. How could I expect my husband even to consider turning over his keys to me? My heart ached just thinking about it. "Dear Lord," I prayed, "How shall I present this to him?"

A few days later, fortified by God's love and the support of my mother and sister, I told Milton that we needed to talk. "Honey, you have such a great legacy in your men's ministry. Please don't let the last thing people remember about you be that you continued driving beyond when it was safe to do so." I alluded to the fact that Milton now had very little feeling in his legs and expressed my concern that because of this he could easily lose control of the car. "Honey, please don't continue to put yourself at risk," I begged. "Please don't take chances that could lead to an accident where others could be injured seriously or even killed."

My husband stared down at his hands the entire time I was speaking, so I had no way to gauge his reaction to what I had said. Now, hardly daring to breathe, I waited for him to respond. Finally he raised his eyes to meet mine, and after hesitating for only a second he said, "Okay." That was it. My wonderful husband who already had lost so much over the last few months, acquiesced to giving up his ability to leave home on his own with a simple okay. I threw my arms around him and hugged and kissed him, relieved that this hurdle was behind us and filled with admiration for this man whom I had married.

After a moment or two, the reality of the situation set in and Milton asked, "How will I get to my physical therapy appointments next week while you are away visiting your mother?"

"We will find a way," I assured him. "Maybe the Monday Night Football Bible study group will help."

A week later, we heard on national news about an elderly gentleman who lost control of his car and plowed through a busy farmer's market, killing ten people and injuring countless others. Milton and I prayed together for all who were involved in that tragic accident, and I added a prayer of thanksgiving that Milton had so unselfishly relinquished his keys.

Remember the old saying, "God never shuts a door without opening a window"? When Milton's physical therapist learned that Milton's weakened legs no longer allowed him to drive using conventional controls, he suggested that we retrofit our car with hand controls. Shortly after that PT visit, we drove to San Diego on a Thursday morning and had my SUV adapted so Milton could drive once again. As we were leaving the shop, one of the managers handed us a business card. "I suggest that you call this woman," he said. "She can give you some helpful tips on how to drive with hand controls." I took the card and thanked him for his suggestion, but my immediate concern was that Milton thought he was going to drive the seventy miles of interstate highway between San Diego and home. I had to persuade him that this wasn't a good idea. I did win that one.

In retrospect, I wish we had taken the manager's advice. But I wish even more that there had been a policy requiring customers to read and sign a release declaring that they understood that a minimum number of hours were required to become proficient in driving with hand controls. As a condition of signing the waiver, the company would be absolved from any damages resulting from driver error.

The crash

The house seemed unusually quiet when I awoke on Saturday morning, and I knew immediately that Milton had taken the car to go practice. I grabbed my Bible, hoping that the familiar words of scripture and a few moments in prayer would calm my fears. I sat down at the kitchen table and, as my mother always strongly suggested, began my reading with Psalm 91. I barely had begun when I heard the garage door open. "Praise God!" I yelled, thankful that I had been spared the agony of anxiously waiting for Milton's return.

My praise was cut short by the sound of the engine revving up to a loud roar. I started toward the laundry room and the door that leads to the garage, but, thankfully, I hadn't gone more than a step or two before I heard and felt the impact of the huge SUV hitting the house with such force that it separated the laundry room door from the wall. The noise of the impact was deafening, but above it I heard the sound of screeching tires and smelled the pungent odor of burning rubber. Milton, it seemed, had used the new hand controls to put the car in reverse at the same time he instinctively placed his foot on the accelerator, catapulting the car out of the garage and across the street where it finally came to a stop upon meeting the immovable force of our neighbors' garage. Noise gave way to a silence even more deafening as I rushed, along with numerous neighbors, to my husband's side.

Milton sat amidst the glass from shattered windows, exclaiming, "It's all my fault. I am so sorry," while a swell of concerned voices reassured him that we were concerned only about his safety. Someone called the paramedics, who arrived quickly and determined that Milton was just fine. In fact, his blood pressure wasn't even elevated. Since Milton was wearing shorts, the paramedics carefully vacuumed the glass around his legs so he wouldn't get cut when they moved him. They helped him out of the vehicle, gave him his walker, and then assisted him into the house. Before leaving, they admonished me not to try and wipe the fine slivers of glass off Milton's skin, but instead to put him in the shower and let the water remove any glass still clinging to his body.

When everything had finally quieted down, I asked Milton, "Are you hurt? Are you cut anywhere?"

He patted himself here and there before replying, "Nope, I don't think I even have a scratch. I feel fine."

How amazing that he survived unscathed from an accident that resulted in one totaled vehicle and considerable damage to two homes! I helped him into bed, but we took time to give thanks to God, before I carefully tucked the covers around him and left him to rest.

The neighbor whose garage had finally stopped the SUV in its tracks surveyed the damage and calmly declared, "It's just brick and mortar. The important thing is that Milt wasn't hurt." The man's gracious comment didn't reflect any of the concern he must have been feeling in light of the fact that he recently had accepted an offer on his home and the sale was scheduled to close on the following Friday. A policeman called to investigate the accident found the palpable kindness in our neighborhood so surreal that he likened it to being transported to La-La land. Our next-door neighbor assured him, "No, you are still in Murrieta, California; these are just Christian people."

I wanted to make sure the kind homeowner remained calm so I hurried home to get the necessary information to assure him that we were well insured and that he would have no trouble getting his garage and front lawn restored in an easy and timely manner. Later that day, I found him outside my garage, and we began talking about what had happened. I told him that I was just sitting down to read my Bible when the crash occurred. His next comment astounded me. "Try reading Psalm 91," he said. Why, that was the very psalm I had been reading! A wonderful calm came over me. I felt the presence of Jesus telling me, "Don't worry Wanda, I *will* take care of you."

People who know me, and my flair for the dramatic, tell me that they marveled at how calm I remained throughout that whole episode. I know that my calm demeanor was a reflection of the inner peace I felt because I had been delivered a message of hope and assurance that, no matter what happened on this journey Milton and I were on together, God would take care of both of us. God always has and I am confident that he will continue to do so.

I'm convinced that if I hadn't heeded my mother's advice to read Psalm 91 all these years, I would have missed hearing God's message to me on the day of Milton's accident—a message that has carried me through many difficult moments in this journey of faith.

Wanda's Story of Caring Family & Friends

Our grandson, Conner, was three years old at the time of Milton's accident. He lived with his family in Washington state. When I called to tell our daughter, Shelly, about the accident, she immediately asked, "What time did all of this happen, Mom?" When I told her, a long silence ensued before she replied, "Mom, you are not going to believe this—Conner and I were walking home from the grocery store this morning when suddenly he stopped dead in his tracks. 'Where is Opa?'" he asked. (Jay, our firstborn grandson lives in Germany and calls us Opa and Oma, so Conner calls us Opa and Oma, the German words for grandfather and grandmother.) Shelly went on to say that she had looked around to see why Conner might have asked the question but she didn't see anything to trigger an association. She also was surprised at Conner's question because he hadn't seen his grandpa since Milton was in the hospital the previous February, and it was now July.

"What did you tell him?" I asked.

"I told him that Opa is at home." Shelly continued, "But Conner wasn't satisfied with that answer. He wanted to know which home. When I replied that Opa was at his California home—the one we visited last summer—Conner wanted to know where Oma was. When I told him you were also at home, he asked the same strange question about which home. I explained that you also were at home in Murietta with Opa. After that he shrugged his little shoulders as if something wasn't quite right about the information I had given him, and then he started walking again without saying another word."

I wonder if Conner sensed something of what was happening to us. Did he think we had gone on to our heavenly home in the accident that destroyed parts of our earthly abode? I smiled, thinking of other instances when it seemed that Conner had a special connection with God. Conner's uncanny concern for us at that very moment left me without a doubt that God would take care of me so I could take care of Milton.

Milt's Story of Caring Family & Friends

Our grandson turned three while visiting us during the summer of my deteriorating health. I wanted to do something special for Conner's birthday and decided I would build him a sandbox. It would be a well-built sandbox, free from splinters and exposed nails. It would be a safe place for Conner to play happily while Opa and Oma watched. I recall thinking, as I headed off to the local hardware store to purchase lumber and sand, that this would be a fairly easy task, but I soon discovered otherwise. The steadily increasing weakness in my legs made the task so difficult that I considered giving up on the plan and doing something else for Conner. But then I would remember how excited Conner had been when I told him about the sandbox, and that would give me the encouragement I needed to continue on even when the project took longer to complete than I had planned and required more strength than I thought I had.

The half-inch plywood that I used to assemble the box became heavier and more awkward for me to handle as I worked slowly in our hot and stuffy garage. As I worked, I was reminded of my time in Mexico mixing cement by hand to lay the foundation for a new home. By the third day, the sandbox was complete and ready to be filled with sand. Since by now I lacked the strength to move the ten-pound bags of sand in one load, I moved them one by one from the back of the SUV, into the wheelbarrow, and then to the courtyard where the sandbox was located. It took me five long trips to accomplish the task of filling Conner's beautiful new sky blue sandbox. All the while, Conner waited eagerly for the moment when he could finally play in the sandbox that Opa built just for him. Conner and I both learned something about patience from that project—and about being blessed. Conner spent countless hours in the sandbox. Watching him play, I felt a special connection between this wonderful child and myself.

Caregiver Tips from Wanda

- Share your stories with each other to enhance understanding, compassion, patience, and love.

- Talk with family and friends to get their perspectives.

- Be creative; words are not the only way to tell a story. Add pictures of family and friends, especially pictures of a favorite group activity. Video cameras, scrapbooking materials, and tape recorders are good resources to use in telling your stories.

Care Receiver Tips from Milt

- Tell your story. I can't believe how cathartic it was for me.

- Share stories about family and friends who are part of your story.

- Be innovative—if you can't use a keyboard, then use a tape recorder or a voice activated computer program

Your Faith Journey

*"It is God who arms me with strength
and makes my way perfect" (Psalm 18:32).*

Record some of the special events and memories of your faith
walk so you can share your story with others.

Who would want to read your story?

Who would benefit from your experiences?

What would your message be?

In what ways have special family and friends
provided support to you in your faith?
What lessons have you learned along the way?

What insights do you have to share with other caregivers?

Prayer requests

Answered prayers

Your Faith Journey

*"It is God who arms me with strength,
and makes my way perfect" (Psalm 18:32).*

Record some of the special events and memories
of your faith walk so you can share your story with others.

Who would want to read your story?

Who would benefit from your experiences?

What would your message be?

In what ways have special family and friends
provided support to you in your faith?

What lessons have you learned along the way?

What insights do you have to share with other care receivers?

Prayer requests

Answered prayers

Step Two

Face Your Fears and Then Take Action

"For I am the LORD, your God, who takes hold of your right

hand and says to you, Do not fear; I will help you" (Isaiah

Wanda's Story

Fear would come upon me often, stealing in like a dreaded intruder. I first felt fear when Milton's weakness and muscle loss began to rapidly escalate after his hospitalization in Seattle. I was not prepared to deal with his declining health nor the potential impact it would have on our lives. I was overwhelmed with fears about the cause of his weakness—was it cancer?—and his prognosis—would he die? How would I cope if Milton suffered a lingering or painful death? Fear intruded most boldly at night, catching me when I was alone and vulnerable, exhausted from the day's activities. In its merciless grip, I would think despairingly about how I would manage if Milton died or became totally incapacitated. By this time, Milton was experiencing extreme nerve pain in his legs for hours at a time. I worried about what he would do when he could no longer stand the pain. When our wonderful doctor, Kelly McKerahan, prescribed an effective pain medication, I began to fear the day would come when the medicine would no longer be effective. In a very real sense, fear was holding me hostage. At times, my heart would race for no apparent reason, and I struggled to catch my breath.

Although it involved a Herculean effort on his part, Milton continued to work full time. However, he now worked out of our home. Still, I worried about what we would do if his employer decided to terminate him. Milton is a big man, and throughout our almost forty years of marriage I had felt secure knowing my big, strong husband would protect me. But now I worried about what *we* would do if a flesh and blood intruder invaded our home.

In truth, I think both Milton and I were living in denial in those days, weeks, and months before his condition was diagnosed. Since we didn't know what to do, we responded to each new fear by pasting on a confident, happy face as we struggled mightily to get through each day. To do otherwise would be to give in to the fear.

Milt's Story

It is easy to understand Wanda's fear of the unknown regarding my condition. Prior to my jury duty stint, I also had concerns about my condition. I wanted answers to several basic questions: Why wasn't I getting better? Was my condition permanent? Would I feel like this for the rest of my life? What adjustments would I need to make to live a normal life? Without answers, I pretended that everything was all right in hopes that it would be. In retrospect, I think I believed that the pain would go away soon, and that was my main concern at the time.

In spite of the intense pain in my feet, I persevered with my daily exercise routine. Being a former athlete, I had endured pain before. What's the old saying? No pain, no gain? So I lived as best as I could with the ebb and flow of pain.

Having been blessed with good health for most of my life, I don't think I truly realized the gravity of my situation. Perhaps if I had been more fearful I would have taken action sooner. We will never know. But what I do know is that my summons to appear for jury duty was pivotal in my struggle not to give in to pain or fear. Jury duty gave me the information I needed to begin developing a plan of action, and any fear I may have had went away as soon as I had a plan in place for how to go about diagnosing and treating my condition.

We now know that I have Chronic Inflammatory Demyelinating Polyneuropathy. CIDP is a relapsing condition, meaning there are good times and bad times. After the initial onset, for example, when I was hospitalized in Seattle, my feet were never an issue. I had not connected the trip to Mexico with the fall in Seattle. That revelation would come much later.

Wanda's Story of Caring Family & Friends

Shelly and I talked on the phone often, so on one level she knew what she would find when she flew into California for a visit during the first part of June. I had intended to meet her at the airport but had a flat tire on the way, so Shelly ended up taking a taxi to our home and arrived before I did. In spite of our phone conversations, Shelly wasn't prepared for the shock of seeing her father struggling with a walker as he hurried as best he could to greet her. All her life Shelly had looked to her big, strong father to protect her. Now he couldn't even help carry her bags into the house. She was used to seeing her distinguished father dressed in a business suit and tie, not shuffling behind a walker. Shelly told me that her first thought was, "I hope Mom gets her tire fixed and returns home soon. I can't deal with this."

Shelly stuck very close to me during her visit, hoping, perhaps, that I could shelter her from having to confront the gravity of the situation. Only after she had returned home to Seattle did she tell me what had happened one day while I was napping. "Dad called me to help him transfer from the recliner to the wheelchair," she said. "We tried for half an hour without success, until I watched him give up and slump back into his chair. I had never seen Dad give up on anything. 'Go get your mother,' he told me in a raspy voice that didn't sound anything like Dad's. I remember feeling so sad for him, knowing he couldn't care for himself anymore. But I also felt sad for you, Mom, as I finally realized just how different your life was going to be from now on. I looked around and was terrified at what I didn't see. Where were the ramps and safety railings that Dad needed? Why wasn't Dad doing physical therapy? It suddenly occurred to me that you and Dad had to be in denial about the whole situation. It was such a shock to me, Mom. I didn't know what to do," she sobbed.

At that moment I wanted so much to comfort my little girl. "Shelly, your dad and I were doing the best we could," I said. "And we were trusting that God would make up the difference."

Milt's Story of Caring Family & Friends

Our son, Milton Scott, came to stay with me one weekend while Wanda attended a women's convention out of town. Although he had volunteered to come as soon as he heard that Wanda was concerned about finding someone to stay with me while she traveled, I also suspected that his mother had assigned him to this task. Wanda had hardly left my side since I became incapacitated, so I am sure she was apprehensive about leaving me for a whole weekend. Milton Scott already had some experience from a prior visit. On that occasion, Wanda came home from running an errand to find him helping me into the bathroom. She rushed to take over, only to be reassured, "Don't worry. Pops and I've got it." And we did. She couldn't have picked a better person to stay with me than our son.

Milton Scott arrived a day before Wanda left and spent that time learning what he needed to do to help me and to keep his mother from worrying. Wanda later confided in me how surprised she was to see what a great caregiver Milton Scott was. Wanda was right. Milton Scott and I had a great time together, and I was proud of his maturity as a young man. He lives in Las

Vegas, and it wasn't convenient for him to set aside his work to come and take care of me. But, even though he had his laptop and cell phone readily available at our home, he didn't use them because he wanted his mother to know that he was giving me his full attention. I was pleased to report to Wanda that she could be proud of her son for doing an outstanding job. We spent a lot of time reminiscing, listening to good jazz, and talking about his recent decision to accept Christ. Milton Scott, although raised in the church, became a Christian on his thirtieth birthday. And I was grateful to think that after all those years of caring for Milton Scott, he was now caring for me. What a blessing.

Caregiver Tips from Wanda

- Acknowledge your fears. Share them with a supportive person.

- Listen when family and friends express concerns about your situation. Carefully consider their concerns and their suggestions. If they make sense, act on them.

- Make new plans for your safety. Draw up a list of neighbors who could be called in case of an emergency.

- Have open and honest discussions about finances with the person for whom you are giving care.

- Search the Bible for assurances from God. The book of Psalms is a great place to start.

- Ask family and friends to share scripture verses that have sustained them through difficult times. Read the verses in your time of need

- Start each day with devotions and prayer. Give thanks daily for God's presence in your life and the special people God sends to help you.

Care Receiver Tips from Milt

- Acknowledge your caregiver's concerns.

- Recognize your fears, but don't be paralyzed by them.

- Arm yourself with all the facts available. Talk to your doctors, read available literature, and seek out the experiences of those in the same situation.

- Remember how to spell fear: *F*alse *E*vidence *A*ppearing *R*eal.

- Remember that God keeps his promises. Know that you are never alone.

Caregiver's Journal

Dealing with Your Fear

"Know therefore that the LORD your God is God;
he is the faithful God, keeping his covenant of love
to a thousand generations of those who love him
and keep his commands" (Deuteronomy 7:9).

Tell about a time when you were afraid and the action
you took to overcome your fear.

In what ways did family and friends provide support?

What lessons did you learn from the experience?

What insights do you have to share with other caregivers?

Prayer requests

Answered prayers

Dealing with Your Fear

"Know therefore that the LORD your God is God;
he is the faithful God, keeping his covenant of love
to a thousand generations of those who love him
and keep his commands" (Deuteronomy 7:9).

Record a time when you've been afraid
and the action you took to overcome those fears.

In what ways did family and friends provide support?

What lessons did you learn from the experience?

What insights do you have to share with other care receivers?

Prayer requests

Answered prayers

Step Three

Choose Great Role Models

"I can do everything through [Christ] who gives me strength"

(Philippians 4:13).

Wanda's Story

Milton is a big guy, and it required a tremendous amount of physical effort on my part to care for him during the worst of our ordeal. "Each one of these legs must weigh a ton," I thought as I moved my husband's paralyzed legs onto the bed each night and back into his chair each morning. I huffed and puffed as I struggled to put on thigh high compression hose that were so tight they made putting on my panty hose seem like a dream. And I prayed for strength as I helped Milton to a standing position so he could transfer from his wheelchair to the car during trips to the doctor or the physical therapist.

Sunday mornings were especially challenging. I would shower and partially dress before helping Milton with his clothing. Then I would finish dressing myself. This routine kept me from becoming soaking wet from the exertion of dressing Milton. By 6:00 A.M. I would be on my way to prepare for playing for the 8:00 A.M. worship service at our church.

I look back on those days and I realize that I literally was running back and forth between making sure Milton had everything he needed and taking care of my own life apart from the life we shared. I remember thinking often during that period, "I got through today, just barely. But how will I have the strength to get through tomorrow . . . and the day after that?"

I also remember that it was at this point that I began noticing particular people—women pushing their husbands in wheelchairs or walking slowly beside them with outstretched hands ready to give support if needed. "They look a lot like me," I thought. When we went to the doctor's office, or physical therapist's, or even out for dinner, I noticed men gently caring for their wives. I began in time to look for caregivers—men or women who appeared to be older than I—and I would tell myself that if they could do this, so could I. These people became my roles models, and when I didn't feel I had another ounce of energy to give, I would think of them and take heart. "I can do that" became a litany for me.

Milt's Story

My cousin Eddie had cerebral palsy. He was a year older than I and lived in my mother's hometown of Carrollton, Missouri. Since Carrollton was sixty miles from where we lived in Kansas City, I didn't see Eddie very often, but he was always upbeat on those occasions when we did get together. Eddie had difficulty getting around and often was hard to understand, but his attitude was always uplifting for those around him. He never complained or asked, "Why me?" It was physically impossible for him to stand erect, but he always stood tall in his mind. While we wanted to feel sorry for Eddie, he never let us.

I guess some of Eddie's attitude rubbed off on me, enabling me to continue to see myself as the man I was even as my body grew steadily weaker and I regressed from walking with a limp to having to use a wheelchair to get around. Was Eddie my role model? Yes, he was! Even in his frail condition, he was an example of what it meant to accept what life hands you and remain positive.

John Deavitt, a member of our Monday night group, suffered from several illnesses and was small in stature, but big in heart. We often marveled at John's positive attitude as he struggled to breathe with the help of a steady supply of oxygen from a tank he carried with him. John was an active member of our group and often gave profound testimony about his faith in Jesus Christ. John also was the first of my Monday night brothers to go home to be with the Lord, leaving behind an indelible impression on all of our lives. Following his funeral, John's sister, Claire, sent me a beautiful book in which she inscribed these words, "To my brother's care group leader: Milton . . . thank you for loving him into the Kingdom."

Eddie and John both showed me how to live in pain and suffering with dignity and without self-pity. Adopting their positive attitudes freed me to focus on the challenges I wanted to master rather than the limitations I currently faced. In my mind, I am always walking. I thank God for Eddie and John's witness.

Wanda's Story of Caring Family & Friends

Tony was everywhere—laughing, working, and then moving on to his next project or appointment. He appeared at our door promptly at 6:30 A.M. every Friday morning for men's Bible study. After that he joined the crew of volunteers who met at the church on Fridays to fold and staple the bulletins for Sunday morning worship. Then he was off for brunch with the guys before picking up his lovely wife, Sylvia, for a doctor's appointment or a physical therapy session or both. Tony also loves children and they love him. He helps with vacation Bible school at our church and it is delightful to watch the little ones run to greet him and get a big bear hug from Mr. C.

Awed by his energy and his enthusiasm, I once asked Tony, "How do you do all that you do and still keep going?"

"You just do what you have to do and pray a lot," he responded. "I'm a few years older than you are, Wanda. If I can do it, you can do it," he laughed. And he was off.

I caught Tony some months later, and in a quieter moment he offered me this advice: "Patience is so important in what we do as caregivers. It is taking the time to look at things from the point of view of the person for whom you are caring. It also helps to have a great sense of humor. If I can remember to laugh, then I think I can get through almost anything. I also try to take care of myself. Recently I decided I needed to lose some weight because I knew I would feel better and it would be good for my body. So I began eating smaller portions and healthier foods. I also started walking to get some exercise. I've lost quite a bit of weight and I feel great! Being a good caregiver is about taking good care of the other person *and* yourself."

Tony is a great role model for me.

Milt's Story of Caring Family & Friends

For more than two years, Larry, aka "Cowboy," came by every morning, weather permitting, to walk with me. It began one day after Cowboy saw me take a few steps using my walker. He was overjoyed that I might one day walk again, and he understood that to attain that goal I would need to build up my endurance. Larry had watched his father remain sedentary in his final years, and he was dedicated to keeping me on my feet and active.

I actually looked forward to those early morning get-togethers with Cowboy. We began by walking from our family room, through the kitchen, down the hall, and back to the family room. We kept track of our progress on a sheet provided by my nurse, Stefanie. Once I could do two or three rounds in the house, we moved outside. At first we made one loop around the out-side of the house, but gradually we progressed to four loops each morning. All the while we walked, we talked, discussing our faith in Jesus Christ, our families, our work, and a whole host of other topics requiring our attention, including the Monday night and Friday morning Bible study groups to which we both belonged.

Although he prefers to be called Cowboy, I think of Larry as "Coach." Since I was pretty much homebound, every opportunity to spend time with another man was priceless to me. In early 2005, Cowboy was diagnosed with leukemia, but his commitment to our morning walk didn't waver until he was finally too ill to continue. Throughout the most difficult times, our Monday night group ministered to Cowboy. We called him when he was too sick to come to Bible study, and, of course, we prayed for him without ceasing. Another friend, Howard, organized a blood drive. We all piled in cars—yes, even me—and with the help of his lovely wife and caregiver, Donna, we surprised him with a visit on his birthday. As I write this book, Cowboy is in remission and is once again involved in our Bible study groups. What a blessing we have been to each other during our illnesses.

Caregiver Tips from Wanda

- Identify people in situations similar to yours who would make good role models. Talk with them about their stories, their challenges, and their tips for success.

- Establish a support system with others. Share with them your joys and concerns and provide a listening ear for theirs.

- Begin thinking and acting as if others might be looking to *you* as a role model

- Write affirming scripture verses on note cards and place them around your home. They can be an inspiration to you as you go through the day.

Care Receiver Tips from Milt

- Surround yourself with positive role models.

- Remember that others may be blessed by your affliction and how you respond to it. Your affliction can somehow be a blessing to others.

- Work at staying positive, despite your current situation. Look to your role models and to the Lord for support and encouragement.

Your Role Models

*"He gives strength to the weary and increases
the power of the weak" (Isaiah 40:29).*

Record stories of other caregivers you have admired.

How have family and friends acted
as positive role models for you?

What lessons have you learned about choosing role models
or about being a role model for someone else?

What insights do you have to share with other caregivers?

Prayer requests

Answered prayers

Your Role Models

"He gives strength to the weary and increases the power of the weak" (Isaiah 40:29).

Record stories of other care receivers you have admired.

How have family and friends acted
as positive role models for you?

What lessons have you learned about choosing role models
or about being a role model for someone else?

What insights do you have to share with other care receivers?

Prayer requests

Answered prayers

Step Four

Acknowledge the Psychological Impact and Keep a Positive Attitude

"Why are you downcast, O my soul? Why so disturbed

within me? Put your hope in God, for I will yet praise him,

my Savior and my God" (Psalm 42:11).

Wanda's Story

As Milton's care claimed more and more of my time and energy, I began to wonder, "Who am I? Am I still Wanda Scott Bledsoe, or am I Wanda, the wife of Milton who is in a wheelchair?" I used to be the one who offered assistance to people with disabilities. Now I found myself striving to be gracious and pleasant when strangers asked if they could help us. Milton's illness also necessitated making changes to our home. I watched carefully as Cecil and Howard, brothers in Christ from the Monday night Bible study group, hammered away at the ramps to help Milton navigate the entry doors to our home. They covered them with beautiful green indoor/outdoor carpet, but I still found them jarring. I had never imagined that our home would need such accommodations. Ramps were for people in wheelchairs, and now that included my husband.

The week Milton was hospitalized to begin his infusion therapy, I had safety rails installed in the master bath and the bathroom in Milton's office. The guest bathroom was too small for

Milton to access with a wheelchair, so I reasoned that it wouldn't be necessary to modify that room. The truth of the matter is that I wanted to retain some parts of our home just as they were to remind me of the way we had lived before.

Throughout my life, God had provided me with an endless array of wonderful experiences, and I never once had thought to ask, "Why me, Lord?" I knew that now was not the time to ask that question because I knew that God wasn't responsible for Milton's condition. Whenever I felt myself getting down, I immediately would start counting my blessings. I included little things, such as a friend from church dropping by with lunch to share, as well as big things like the notice from our insurance company that thousands of dollars in medical costs would be covered completely. I was amazed at how much better I felt after I had listed at least ten ways God had blessed me that day. Some may call it "the power of positive thinking." I call it "the joy and peace that comes from counting God's blessings."

Milt's Story

As I tool around our home in my power chair, I count my blessings, including the fact that a year before my trip to Mexico, we moved from a two-story house to the single-story we now call home. This clearly is a blessing because as my condition worsened, it would have been impossible for me to climb the stairs to the master bedroom in the old house. Who knew that a year after moving into this smaller home with laminate flooring that my immune system would attack the nerve linings in my legs and I would find myself in a wheelchair? Who knew what a blessing that strange looking laminate floor would be as Wanda pushed me easily across its smooth surface? Who knew how much I would need that smooth surface as I took my first faltering steps using a walker? We didn't, but God did. The ramps and the safety rails Wanda had installed allow me to move about safely with relative ease. But even in this more "user friendly" house, it often requires multiple trips to move items from one area to another. And every trip requires prior planning. Do I have my cell phone? What's my back up in case of an emergency?

The bottom line is that now I need to be careful and make the right choices about things I once took for granted. By keeping a positive attitude, I am able to accomplish so much more. Wanda tells me that my positive attitude is a tremendous help in her efforts to stay optimistic. I think we agree that maintaining a positive attitude is energizing and allows hope to be ever present, while negativity drains hope. I look forward to the challenges involved in performing menial tasks such as moving our three large trash barrels from the side of the house to the curb every Thursday. Meeting such challenges means a great deal. It means I am improving physically, which in turn means I am getting stronger and more independent. And the psychological benefit that comes with regaining some degree of independence is immeasurable.

Wanda's Story of Caring Family & Friends

We had done this before—worked together to get Milton back up into his wheelchair when he had slipped out. This time was different. Milton's condition had deteriorated since the last time, and no matter what we tried, we couldn't get him off the floor. Finally he told me to call the paramedics to come and help. I glanced at the clock. It was almost two o'clock in the morning. "Oh, Milton, I'm embarrassed to call at this hour." I countered, "Why don't I make you a nice pallet here on the floor? I'll make one for myself right beside you." I knew that the nurse who came in twice a week to administer Milton's infusion therapy would be coming bright and early. "When Stefanie arrives, she will help us get you back in your chair."

Milton's response indicated he didn't like my plan at all. "Just call them, Wanda," he insisted.

I reluctantly made the call, and the paramedics arrived within minutes. I was prepared to begin apologizing profusely as soon as I opened the door, but I didn't get a chance before one of the paramedics said, "I remember this house." Indeed, the three men standing in my home at 2:00 A.M. were the very same paramedics who had attended to Milton after his accident in the SUV the previous summer.

I took them to Milton and we briefly recounted the accident and what a miracle it was that he had escaped without even the tiniest scratch. Then, working as a team, I counted to three and in one effortless movement they lifted Milton into his chair.

"Now, what else can we do for you?" they asked.

"That's it," I replied, "unless you would like to stay for an early breakfast."

"Another time," they promised, and then laughing together, they were off.

As I write this, I think back fondly to that night and whisper a prayer of thanksgiving for the many wonderful healthcare professionals who have made our journey bearable, interesting, and even entertaining. Isn't God good?

Milt's Story of Caring Family & Friends

Fortunately, we have only had to call 911 on rare occasions. However, it is comforting to know that paramedics are ready, willing, and able to assist any time we need them. Our first 911 call was the day I totaled our SUV. The second occurred on a night when I feel asleep in my lounger and dreamed I could walk. Caught up in the dream, I pulled myself up from the lounger, took one step, and fell to the floor. A quick assessment indicated that I was not injured, but for the next hour, Wanda and I tried many ways to get me back into my chair or any chair. I even crawled from our great room to our master bedroom, but could not muster the energy necessary to get up. About 2:00 A.M. we finally called 911. Within moments the paramedics were at our door, and on Wanda's count of three, I was back in my wheelchair.

The three paramedics who came to our aid this time were the same ones who had responded several months earlier when I lost control of our SUV. They remembered how nice everyone had been to them on that occasion and were glad to see me again.

Our third 911 call took place when Wanda was traveling. On that occasion I was enjoying lunch on our back patio when I ran two of my wheelchair wheels off the pavement and onto the grass. Thankfully I had my cell phone with me, because after trying repeatedly to get my chair back on the pavement, I finally had to call for help. I stayed on the phone with the 911 operator until the paramedics arrived. Believe it or not, it was the same crew once again! After joking that we had to stop meeting like this, they quickly got me and my power chair back on the pavement, and we spent a few minutes discussing the upcoming World Series. What a great group of guys these public servants are! They always have been there when we needed them.

Caregiver Tips from Wanda

- Bravely and faithfully face the facts of the change you are encountering by brainstorming with your care receiver ways and ideas for creative adjustments. Include family and friends in your discussion.

- Find reasons to laugh at yourself, with the person for whom you are providing care, and with anyone else who could use a lift.

- Keep a book of funny sayings close at hand. Read one a day or as needed.

- Learn to accept your feelings, to openly explore them, and to share them with others.

- Find a good listener with whom you can share your deepest feelings without being judged. A good listener is very important to my sense of well-being. I found it helped immensely when I could talk about my feelings and have the other person just say, "Uh-huh, yes, I'm listening," without trying to tell me I shouldn't feel this way or suggesting solutions to my problem. A good listener is a special gift from God, someone who blesses us with love, time, and that listening ear we need so much.

Care Receiver Tips from Milt

- Try to keep a sense of humor and stay focused on the positive. Surround yourself with people who have a positive attitude.

- Be willing to try new approaches. Look for ways to turn a negative situation into something positive.

- Remember to say thank you to everyone who lends a helping hand.

Caregiver's Journal

Dealing with Change

"Surely then you will find delight in the Almighty and will lift up your face to God" (Job 22:26).

Write about the changes that have hit you the hardest.

Record a recent situation that made you laugh.

In what ways have family and friends helped you to have a positive outlook?

What have you learned about staying positive?

What insights do you have to share with other caregivers?

Prayer requests

Answered prayers

Dealing with Change

"Surely then you will find delight in the Almighty and will lift up your face to God" (Job 22:26).

Write about the changes that have hit you the hardest.

Record a recent situation that made you laugh.

In what ways have family and friends helped you to have a positive outlook?

What have you learned about staying positive?

What insights do you have to share with other care receivers?

Prayer requests

Answered prayers

Step Five

Pace Yourself

"Whether you turn to the right or to the left, your ears

will hear a voice behind you, saying, 'This is the way;

walk in it'" (Isaiah 30:21).

Wanda's Story

From the beginning of Milton's illness, my mother's advice has been to pace myself for the long haul. At first I didn't heed her wise words and sprinted through each day like "Superwoman" loose in the neighborhood. Prior to the diagnosis of Milton's illness, our days were filled with endless doctor appointments and physical therapy sessions in our home. After a diagnosis was made, Stefanie, our nurse, began coming to our home twice a week to administer Milton's infusion therapy. These were the best of times. Milton was receiving wonderful care and was starting to show some improvement. But the effort of getting him *and* me ready each day was exhausting, and having so many healthcare professionals in our home took its toll on our privacy.

What a whirlwind life I led! Between attending to Milton's needs and pursuing my responsibilities outside of our home, I felt some days like a hamster running endlessly on a wheel in a cage. I quickly learned how important it was to start my day with God. After giving thanks for the ways God had blessed us the previous day, I would present my "To Do" list for this day and ask God to bless it and divinely order it. I was able to publish my daily devotional *His Roses & Thorns* the first year of Milton's illness because God's grace allowed me to do the work of three people, which was just the number needed on most days. I learned to schedule the tasks I least enjoyed for early morning when I was fresh. And I posted a saying on my computer that my mother suggested I use: "Good Morning, This is God. I will be handling all of your problems today. I will not need your help. So relax and have a great day." I have countless stories of instances when that reminder helped me let go and let God, and of the wonderful results that ensued.

Milt's Story

Each day takes less and less effort to get through. However, in the beginning, when I was on so many medications, it seemed as if everything required more effort and more energy than I had to give. In addition, I felt as if my mind wasn't working right. I seemed to be operating in a fog. So I did what I could and I didn't worry about the rest. Wanda helped a great deal by making sure that we always set aside plenty of time to get ready for appointments. I appreciated the fact that she didn't try to rush me. One of the things I really tried to avoid was anything that made me feel stressed. I also found I needed more time than usual to process information. Wanda understood that and would help communicate to health care professionals that I might need several days to think about a new procedure or a new schedule. I also gave myself permission to do only as much as I could, and nothing more. This was especially the case before I was given a pain patch to manage the severe pain I was experiencing, pain that drained me of all my energy and left me unable to do much at all.

Often when the Men's Monday Night Football Bible study group was here, I would start out the evening with them, but about halfway through I would leave the men and Wanda would help me get into bed. The men would finish the study, clean up the kitchen from the meal we took turns providing, turn off the lights, and leave, locking the doors behind them. These men knew the fellowship meant so much to me that they offered to gather on and around the bed so we could finish the evening together. Wanda and I both laughed and said, "Maybe not."

Pacing myself meant breaking tasks up into small pieces, and it meant being honest in admitting when I just wasn't feeling up to doing a particular task. Wanda needed to pace herself as she tried to manage two lives—hers and mine. I was forced to pace myself because my body and my mind seemed to shut down if I didn't.

Wanda's Story of Caring Family & Friends

Stefanie was an answer to prayer. I asked God to send us someone who could insert an IV on the first try so Milton wouldn't have to endure repeated needle sticks, but God gave us so much more. Stefanie provided us with information about Milton's condition and advised us to have a "port-a-cath" implanted in his shoulder when his veins could no longer endure the twice a week IV infusions. She also accompanied Milton to his neurologist's office to help with a spinal tap, a difficult procedure made even more so because of Milton's limited mobility. The physician was grateful for her assistance, and so were we.

Stefanie brought so much of herself into our home. It was as if God sent her to coordinate all aspects of Milton's care, from interpreting his lab results to reviewing physical therapy progress notes and physician recommendations. One of her greatest gifts to us was her offer to provide the essential foot care Milton needed. This selfless act of love saved us precious time and energy that we would have spent going to a podiatrist's office. We were also the recipients of Stefanie's love of cooking and gardening. Her peach preserves were absolutely delicious. And even my mother became an ardent fan when she heard Stefanie had brought tomato plants and the stakes necessary to keep the vines off the ground once *she* had planted them. What a treat to have our own homegrown tomatoes for the first time in our nearly forty years of marriage. What fun it was to check on their progress when Stefanie came for Milton's treatment. And what joy it was to eat delicious salads tossed with our tomatoes and Stefanie's love and care! I asked for a skilled nurse and God lavishly blessed us with Stefanie.

Milt's Story of Caring Family & Friends

We got to know our new neighbors, Tom and Rosa, at the annual neighborhood open house we hosted each Christmas. In the course of our conversation that evening, we learned that Tom was a career medical-surgical nurse in the US Navy. We couldn't believe it. Wanda and I had been looking for some time for someone to come in and help me shower once a week. We had called a number of agencies, but the services they offered didn't seem to fit our specific needs. Because my illness had robbed me of so much privacy, I truly hoped we could find a male attendant to help me with my personal care. Now God had provided an answer to prayer right in our own neighborhood!

"Would you consider providing my personal care?" I asked Tom, hopefully.

"I would be glad to," Tom replied.

It was the beginning of a great friendship. Tom came over each Saturday morning, and what began as a half hour task evolved into a half day opportunity for male bonding over jazz music and conversation about current events and matters of faith. We had a ball.

At first, Tom attended to my personal care while I sat on a stool in the shower. But when he learned, all too soon, that he and his family were being transferred to a military base in Japan, Tom began to teach me how I could safely attend to my own personal care. I remember proudly the glorious day when Tom and I announced that I could now lift my leg over the shower door frame, stand, and shower by myself. Yes!

We continue to give thanks for Tom and his wife Rosa for sharing him with us on those blessed Saturday mornings. I miss Tom and our Saturday mornings very much, and I will never forget his care and devotion.

Caregiver Tips from Wanda

- Don't over-schedule. Remember that you cannot do everything. Instead, prioritize your life as well as your day. Try to do the really important things and not worry if the items at the bottom of the list don't get done.

- Make use of your computer to store information so it is readily accessible.

- Look for ways the same information can be copied to different medical documents that have been requested.

- Ask people who have special knowledge or gifts of dealing with insurance and medical related issues for help in these areas.

- Keep a folder handy and ask healthcare providers for copies of their assessments and documentation. Ask for written instructions for procedures you don't quite understand.

- Don't hesitate to ask a healthcare provider to suggest someone who could provide a second opinion, if you want one.

Care Receiver Tips from Milt

- Be honest about what you feel like doing and what you don't.

- Realize that what you can do may vary from day to day.

- Communicate honestly with your caregiver and other family and friends.

- Recognize what causes you stress and avoid it as much as possible.

Caregiver's Journal

Pacing Yourself

"I will instruct you and teach you in the way you should go; I will counsel you and watch over you" (Psalm 32:8).

What task do you like least? Invite someone to brainstorm with you ways you can make the task more agreeable.

Who helped make sure that you saw the right healthcare professionals and that your views were heard? How did they help you?

What healthcare professionals stand out in your experience? Why are they memorable?

What have you learned about pacing yourself?

What insights do you have to share with other caregivers?

Prayer requests

Answered prayers

Pacing Yourself

"I will instruct you and teach you in the way you should go; I will counsel you and watch over you" (Psalm 32:8).

What task do you like least? Invite someone to brainstorm with you ways you can make the task more agreeable.

Who helped make sure that you saw
the right healthcare professionals and that
your views were heard? How did they help you?

What healthcare professionals stand out in your experience?
Why are they memorable?

What have you learned about pacing yourself?

What insights do you have to share with other care receivers?

Prayer requests

Answered prayers

Step Six

Develop a Good Support System

"And we know that in all things God works for the good of those

who love him, who have been called according to his purpose"

(Romans 8:28).

Wanda's Story

When we moved to Temecula more than ten years ago, we joined Hope Lutheran Church and jumped in with both feet. We have come to think of our congregation as our extended family. When Milton got sick, our Hope family was right there for us, offering every kind of support that you could imagine.

We moved into a new home and neighborhood just a year before Milton's illness struck, but next-door neighbors, Ber and Saundra, made sure we felt at home right away. They hosted an open house to welcome us and help us get acquainted with the neighborhood. We reciprocated the following Christmas by hosting an open house of our own. When Milton got sick we discovered that our neighbors were also right there for us. Saundra and Ber didn't even take time to change out of their pajamas when I frantically called them early one morning, saying please come and help me lift Milton after a fall. That very afternoon, our neurologist admitted Milton into the hospital.

Our support network extended well beyond our church and neighborhood. My mother and sister called daily and our adult children checked in with visits and phone calls. Janice, my hairstylist, came to the house when I couldn't go to her, and she even prepared our Christmas dinner one year when I just didn't have the emotional or physical strength to face cooking for our extended family. Oh, how we enjoyed Janice's Louisiana gumbo and having her daughter, who looks and *sounds* like Natalie Cole, sing for us!

Milton and I marvel at how truly blessed we are to have such a wonderful support network of caring family and friends.

Milt's Story

Developing a good support system is much like putting together a good athletic team. You need the right talent and the right players. In our case, the medical team—our family doctor, neurologist, ophthalmologist, occupational and physical therapists, and IVIg nurse—was essential to my ongoing improvement. These folks had the game plan and knew how to execute it. But no team is successful without the players on the special teams. Our special teams included the countless people who prayed for us and the many, many volunteers who cared for us in big and small ways. Cards, letters, phone calls, and visitors arrived from far and near, expressing concern and support for my return to good health.

Our good neighbor, Bob, who has since moved to Florida, provided support in a very unique way. We were having trouble with birds building nests in various nooks and crannies under our eaves and patio cover and on the side of our house. I was successful in evicting the swallow and wrens, but the pigeons were proving to be more than I could handle. As weak as I was, I didn't feel safe standing any higher than on the bottom rung of the ladder. But that wasn't nearly high enough for me to reach the eaves where the pigeons were roosting. As I struggled to climb the next rung of the ladder, Bob suddenly appeared and ordered in no uncertain terms, "Get down from there; you have no business on that ladder!"

He was right, of course. So I dismounted and let Bob take over. Within moments he had completed a task that I had been wrestling with for more than half an hour. Bob's act of kindness probably prevented me from falling and seriously injuring myself. I thank God that Bob was so vigilant and caring during those initial stages of my illness.

Wanda's Story of Caring Family & Friends

I have never belonged to a true support group, yet Moms' Morning Fellowship certainly became that for me. Our daughter, Shelly, belonged to a group of moms with preschoolers at her church in Seattle that could best be described as a combination Bible study, fellowship, and mutual support group. Shelly loved it, and I thought that it would be great to start a similar group at our church. I have for many years felt called and empowered by God to encourage and support women of all ages, and because of that I volunteered to develop and lead what came to be called Mom's Morning Fellowship (MMF). MMF had been in existence for a couple of years when Milton became ill, and from the start that group of moms with preschoolers rallied around "Mother Wanda" in my time of need.

Since there was no way I could leave Milton every Friday morning to attend MMF, one of the moms, Karin, volunteered to lead the group until I could return. I really missed the fellowship and camaraderie with the young moms, and Karin assured me that they missed me too and were eager for me to return. Months passed before I finally felt that Milton was at a place where I could leave him for a few hours to return to Mom's Morning Fellowship.

I was welcomed back into the fold with a surprise sixtieth birthday party and enough love and prayers to last a lifetime. These beautiful women who were decades younger than I had shared my joys, concerns, fears, and frustrations over previous months, even as they continued to support one another. Truly we are kin to one another, beloved children in God's amazing family.

Milt's Story of Caring Family & Friends

Not long after we joined Hope Lutheran Church, Wanda convinced me to attend a get together at the home of our associate pastor followed by a planning meeting for the formation of small groups in the church. I suggested at that time that we form a group for men. Pastor Mericle agreed, and he indicated that I should spearhead it. What little I knew about leading a men's group I had learned during my time with Connie Jacobsen in Seattle. I found myself wondering if this could be the ministry we had prayed I would find when we had gathered for lunch one last time before Wanda and I moved to California.

A few weeks later, in the fall of 1993, we held our first meeting in conjunction with the beginning of the Monday Night Football season. Since then more than forty men have come one week or another to our home to enjoy fellowship, prayer, and Bible study. As our faith grew, so our relationships with one another deepened. The next fall, we began meeting year round and the group of "regulars" grew to nearly twenty men.

In time, we decided to have a men's advance to get the men of the church together for a full day of fellowship. I invited Connie and his assistant Art to Temecula to facilitate the event, which was attended by more than seventy-five men. Now we hold annual advances and the Monday night group continues to meet weekly. These are the men who rallied to support us when I became ill, and they continue to do so in many and various ways to this day. Words are inadequate to express how much we appreciate their acts of kindness, including the installation of overhead shelving in the garage on which to store Christmas decorations from one year to the next. My life, as is Wanda's, is richly blessed by the love and support of these brothers in Christ.

Tips from the Caregiver & the Care Receiver

Caregiver Tips from Wanda

- Renew and strengthen your relationship with God and your church family. If you have not been active in a church, seek out a congregation in which you feel comfortable, welcomed, and loved.

- Ask a friend who is in the healthcare field for help in identifying support services. Your church may also have an established support group to help people in your situation.

- Reach out to family and friends for help when you need it.

- Establish a ritual of reading from a daily devotional. Share this time or some part of this time with the person for whom you are caring.

Care Receiver Tips from Milt

- Always be willing to accept help, even when you think you don't need it.

- Seek the counsel of experts and follow their advice.

- Recognize the importance of a great support group. If one is available, join it. If one is not available, and develop one yourself.

Caregiver's Journal

Developing Your Support System

"The LORD your God is with you, he is mighty to save. He will take great delight in you, he will quiet you with his love, he will rejoice over you with singing" (Zephaniah 3:17).

Look back over your faith journey.
What support system has helped sustain you along the way?

What friends and family members have been
there to support you?

What lessons have you learned about relying on others?

What insights do you have to share with other caregivers?

Prayer requests

Answered prayers

Developing Your Support System

"The LORD *your God is with you, he is mighty to save. He will take great delight in you, he will quiet you with his love, he will rejoice over you with singing" (Zephaniah 3:17).*

Look back over your faith journey.
What support system has helped sustain you along the way?

What friends and family members have been
there to support you?

What lessons have you learned about relying on others?

What insights do you have to share with other care receivers?

Prayer requests

Answered prayers

Step Seven

Call for Help and Care for Those Who Provide It

"Dear children, let us not love with words or tongue but with actions and in truth" (1 John 3:18).

Wanda's Story

I always have prided myself on being one who steps in to help others, but with the onset of Milton's illness, I became the one in need of help. One thing that helped me make peace with my new role was my decision to create a warm and inviting atmosphere in our home so that the many volunteer and professional people who came to our home to help us would find it a pleasant experience.

I had neither time nor energy to do any major cleaning. A wonderful young woman named Lupe came in once a week to do that. My contributions to our home's welcoming atmosphere included lighting vanilla scented candles, or, on chilly days, building a fire in the fireplace. Sometimes I made cookies—the slice-and-bake kind from the grocery case—and offered our helpers a tasty treat still warm from the oven. I opened the blinds wide each morning so the sun could brighten the room. I made a point of telling people how much their gifts of time and energy meant to us, and I often wrote a note of thanks, as well.

Milton and I focused on the positive things happening in our lives. We made sure there was lots of laughter, even though occasionally it was at our expense. People noticed. In fact, the men who did the repairs on our home after Milton's accident remarked about how much fun it was to be around us.

"Why are you always so happy?" they asked.

I just smiled and replied, "Because God is so good."

Initially I found myself evaluating whether or not we really needed the various kinds of help that people offered. Soon I learned to accept help from others in the spirit in which it was offered. The next step—learning to ask for help when we needed something specific—was much more difficult. I didn't like asking for help, but when I saw the joy on the faces of those who came to our aid, I realized that I wasn't the only one who enjoyed helping others. I tried to ask for things I really couldn't do myself and attempted to be flexible in accepting it when it was available. It was quite a learning experience for me. What a blessing to experience anew the wondrous expressions of a loving God!

Milt's Story

I believe that I hesitated to tell Wanda about my condition early on because I wanted to protect her. Knowing her penchant for getting overly involved, I feared that she would respond to my illness by trying to do more than she could handle safely. I was right. As my situation worsened, Wanda assumed more and more responsibility for my care. Finally, I reached the point where I was unable to take care of myself at all. I couldn't put on my socks, shoes, or pants without Wanda's assistance, much less the compression hose that I wore to control the swelling in my feet. Wanda became very good at putting on the skintight hose and all the other things I needed done. I will be eternally grateful for Wanda's attentiveness and commitment to me, but I regret the toll it took on her. I know that that her arms ached from trying to lift me because I would sometimes notice her rubbing them after she had helped transfer me from my bed to my wheelchair. Since she spent most days running from one task to another with very little time to rest, I knew she had to be tired.

Chronic Inflammatory Demyelinating Polyneuropathy (CIDP) is a rare disease affecting one person in 100,000. Full recovery is possible, and that is my goal. I have learned that nerves damaged by CIDP heal at a rate of one millimeter per month, so recovery will take time. My doctors predicted that it would take twelve to eighteen months for me to regain my ability to walk. In less than a year I was walking with the aid of a walker. My motivation to get better as quickly as possible is that I want to spare my beloved wife from being burdened with my care any more than is absolutely necessary. My illness has helped me appreciate what caregivers, like Wanda, endure while tending to the needs of the people they love. I thank God for the miracle of healing that has enabled me to free Wanda from some aspects of my care.

Wanda's Story of Caring Family & Friends

Remember Lupe? Besides cleaning our house once a week, Lupe helped us in other ways as well. As Christmas approached, I knew that I couldn't turn to my husband, who was by this time using a wheelchair, to help me decorate the house for the holidays. Bless her heart, Lupe volunteered to do it, and she recruited others from her family to help. In just over an hour Lupe and her crew accomplished what would have taken me at least two days. But that isn't the end of the story. Lupe's sister, Dora, prepared homemade tamales that we ate amidst conversation and laughter in our festively decorated home. Of course we paid for the tamales and I also paid for the tree decorating assistance. Milt and I are very careful to avoid even the appearance of taking advantages of our "Hispanic family." Now, as a part of an annual tradition for our families, we place an order for Dora's delicious homemade tamales every year.

Two women, both named Mary, can be counted on to play active roles in the life of our church and to be perfectly groomed while doing so. While I admire their beautifully manicured nails and marvel at their perfectly coiffed hair, what draws me to them is the fact that both understand intimately what it means to be a caregiver. One Mary has shared with me her physical and emotional struggle of caring for a dying husband. Another Mary and I have talked about her relationship as a caregiver for her husband who has been ill for several years. I stand in awe of their stamina and their patience, and I cherish their advice to pray often and look to others for encouragement. "You can do it," they assure me. "We're praying for you."

Sister Kathe and Sister Laura are part of our church office staff, but they aren't nuns like their titles suggest. They are my sisters in Christ. I can always depend on them to give me a boost when my spirit is lagging and to give me a little wiggle room when I'm running behind on a deadline for a newsletter article or an announcement for the Sunday bulletin. As I've struggled to keep all my balls in the air during Milton's illness, Sister Kathe and Sister Laura have made it possible for me to continue to do some of the things I love to do at church, while at the same time caring for Milton.

Milt's Story of Caring Family & Friends

Howard has been part of the Monday night men's group longer than anyone other than myself. When it became impossible for me to drive, Howard offered to pick me up for church on Sundays so Wanda, who is our church organist, could continue to go earlier to prepare for the worship service. This arrangement has been going on for more than two years now, and often we attend the monthly men's breakfast at Hope on Saturday, too.

I truly enjoy Howard's friendship and think of him as a brother. He is an excellent caregiver, and I have learned during our rides to and from church that he developed his caregiver skills while caring for his Aunt Edie when he was younger. Like me, Aunt Edie used both a wheelchair and a walker.

Howard's gift for care giving is a blessing to me. Without his assistance and his commitment to my mobility, I wouldn't be able to participate in the church activities that I so enjoy. Our congregation recently moved to a new campus. Howard took it upon himself to check out the new facility in advance to make sure that I would be able to safely maneuver the site with my walker.

Howard doesn't only serve as my chauffeur; he also does maintenance around our house. Wanda's father was a carpenter. I inherited many of his tools, but I haven't been able to use them since I got sick. I'm thankful for Howard's skills, and I am relieved that because of his care for our home, I no longer have to worry about Wanda falling off the ladder while trying to change the air filters. I will be indebted forever to my friend and brother, Howard, for his care and kindness.

Caregiver Tips from Wanda

- God *is* good and gives us choices. You may not have had a choice in what you are experiencing in life, but you do have a choice about how you will endure and persevere.

- Create an inviting atmosphere in your home. Let in as much light and fresh air as possible.

- Be considerate of the time of others when asking for help, and be gracious in accepting help when it was offered.

- Look for creative ways to show your appreciation. Remember always to write a note or call to thank someone who has been especially helpful.

- Meditate on one of my favorite scripture verses: "Before they call I will answer; while they are still speaking I will hear" (Isaiah 65:24). Record in your journal a time when God provided help in abundance *before* you even asked for it.

Care Receiver Tips from Milt

- If you have limited mobility, keep a communication device with you at all times.

- Always be thankful and courteous to those who assist you in your time of need.

Caregiver's Journal

Your Call for Help

"We also rejoice in our sufferings, because we know that suffering produces perseverance; perseverance, character; and character, hope" (Romans 5:3-4).

Recall a time when you asked for and received help
that made a significant impression on you.
What part did God play in the help you received?

What special family and friends have provided help to you?
How have you responded to that help?

What lessons have you learned about asking for
and receiving help from others?

What insights do you have to share with other caregivers?

Prayer requests

Answered prayers

Your Call for Help

"We also rejoice in our sufferings, because we know that suffering produces perseverance; perseverance, character; and character, hope" (Romans 5:3-4).

Recall a time when you asked for and received help
that made a significant impression on you.
What part did God play in the help you received?

What special family and friends have provided help to you?
How have you responded to that help?

What lessons have you learned about asking for
and receiving help from others?

What insights do you have to share with other care receivers?

Prayer requests

Answered prayers

Step Eight

Take Time for Yourself

"And God blessed the seventh day and made it holy, because

on it he rested from all the work of creating that he had done"

(Genesis 2:3).

Wanda's Story

In the early days of our journey together through Milton's illness, I pretty much ignored my own needs. I think I did so in part because of my motherly instincts to attend to the needs of others before my own and also because I was raised with an above-average work ethic. But as we moved further along on our journey, I started to think more about what I needed. I remember on one occasion asking Milton what he needed me to do for him that day, and realizing, as he listed one thing after another, that his needs once again were going to take precedence over anything I had hoped to do. I felt overwhelmed by the enormity of the day's demands, almost as if a heavy weight was driving me little by little into the ground. The voice in my head screamed, "I can't. I won't!"

To his credit, Milton often encouraged me to take care of myself and my needs. My mother and sister also admonished me, saying, "You can't take care of Milton if you are worn out physically and emotionally." It took a while, but finally I realized they were right.

What did I need? "Quiet time" was at the top of my list. To make sure I met this need, I began rising earlier so I could sit and read or putter around the house for a time before helping Milton begin his day.

"More energy" came next on my list. Before long I had figured out that taking a half-hour nap mid-afternoon gave me the boost I needed to get through the evening. I found that it worked well to schedule a nap while Milton worked with the physical therapist or underwent an infusion therapy treatment. Manicures and pedicures can be very relaxing, so I started treating myself to one or the other on a regular basis. As Milton improved and was able to stay by himself for short periods, I began doing things that I loved: conducting Bible studies with young moms, leading workshops, and becoming active in our church's women's organization. Being with people I enjoyed and using my God-given talents helped me feel like me again. I felt energized even though I was busier than ever. Periodically I asked Milton's nurse to take my blood pressure. My "normal" blood pressure reading was all the proof I needed that taking time for myself to meet my needs was working.

Milt's Story

I believe that taking time for myself is essential to my recovery. Wanda might call my insistence on "my time" self-centered. I call it being focused. I need time alone to regroup.

One of my favorite ways to take time for myself is to do crossword puzzles. Not only do they relax me, they help keep my mind sharp. Doing the puzzle in the newspaper each day helped combat the foggy thinking that plagued me at the onset of my illness when I was on so much medication. Completing the puzzle gave me both a sense of accomplishment and assured me that my mental faculties were intact.

I enjoy quality "me" time listening to good jazz. When I first got sick, the music relaxed me and helped me deal with the intense pain in my feet and legs by giving me something other than the pain upon which to focus. Even though Wanda takes issue with some of the programs, I also enjoy watching television, especially the western channel. The old black and white films bring back pleasant memories of my childhood. I like watching sitcoms, too, and the sillier the better, because they make me laugh. Laughing is an important part of the recovery program I've designed for myself. I like to laugh and Wanda grudgingly admits that laughing releases something called endorphins that are actually good for your body.

Since our days are so jam-packed, I have discovered that scheduling time to do nothing is very therapeutic. Wanda is a "Type A" personality—always in motion; always thinking. I am glad when she decides to do something just for herself. Taking time for myself, and making sure that Wanda does the same, is essential to my recovery.

Wanda's Story of Caring Family & Friends

Loralee is a quiet, scholarly woman who approached me after church one Sunday and offered to stay with Milton while I ran errands. I thanked her for her offer but told her that Milton was well enough to stay by himself for short periods. "What I really would appreciate," I told her, "is having someone who would exercise with me." We discovered that we already belonged to the same fitness center, so it was simply a matter of finding a time. Loralee graciously offered to join me over her lunch hour and I accepted. Soon we were meeting regularly. The exercise was good for me, but so was the conversation. Quiet, scholarly Loralee would smile and occasionally nod as I prattled on about this, that, and the other.

Loralee liked to garden, and when I mentioned one day that I needed to add some color to the beds near our front door, she went with me to our local home and garden store and helped me pick out a variety of flowers. Then she spent the afternoon helping me plant them. Actually, my contribution to the effort was to hand Loralee the tools when she requested them. We had a wonderful time, and I was amazed at how much she knew about cultivating flowers. I had no idea that there are so many steps in planting flowers! Loralee has since moved to Florida, but every time I turn into our driveway and see the flowers she planted, I think of my quiet friend and I give thanks that God placed her in my life during the two years when I needed her most.

Milt's Story of Caring Family & Friends

"May we come to see you?" Jean and Gerry, our friends from Ohio, called to ask. "We can stay in a hotel. We will try hard not to be a bother." We could hear the concern in Gerry's voice. "We just need to see for ourselves that you all are all right." And so they came, and of course, they stayed with us in our home. They asked lots of questions, and we told them our story of walking together through my illness. They applauded our accomplishments and offered encouragement for the challenges we still faced.

Jean accompanied Wanda on one of her frequent trips to the medical equipment store, hoping to find something that would enable me to be a little more independent. Jean is a very independent person and she understands my need to do as much on my own as possible. She found a contoured seat cushion that made it easier for me to transfer from my wheelchair to the car seat. Perhaps it seems a small thing, but we saw it as cause for celebration. How happy we were that our friends had come to see us!

Roger, our former pastor, and his wife, Jackie, called from Seattle to say that they wanted to come see us. "We can stay in a hotel," they assured us. "We will try hard not to be a bother." Of course we were glad to have them come, and we insisted they stay at our home. We went to fun restaurants and talked of old times. Roger pushed my wheelchair so Wanda got a break. We loved having our friends visit. It was good to be up close and personal. We especially liked it when Roger and Jackie laid their hands on us and prayed for us. Their visit refreshed us and gave us energy to continue our journey.

Caregiver Tips from Wanda

- Make a list of the things that refresh and renew your spirit. Think outside the box about how to make them happen. Be flexible.

- Try yoga or relaxation exercises.

- Call a friend to join you for early morning walks. If the weather doesn't cooperate, try walking in a nearby mall.

- Join a caregivers' support group, or start one of your own.

- Engage the advice and help of family and friends; *especially* the one for whom you are caring.

Care Receiver Tips from Milt

- Take time to enjoy family and friends.

- Celebrate little things.

- Do things that you really enjoy even if they don't make sense to anyone else.

- Try something new that you may end up enjoying.

- Take time to do nothing—you deserve it!

Caregiver's Journal

Take Time for Yourself

*The apostles gathered around Jesus and reported to him
all they had done and taught. Then, because so many people
were coming and going that they did not even have a chance to
eat, he said to them, "Come with me by yourselves to a quiet
place and get some rest" (Mark 6:30-31).*

How did you come to realize the importance
of taking care of yourself? What did you do about it?

How did family and friends help you take care of yourself?

What did you learn about taking time for yourself?

What insights do you have to share with other caregivers?

Prayer requests

Answered prayers

Take Time for Yourself

The apostles gathered around Jesus and reported to him all they had done and taught. Then, because so many people were coming and going that they did not even have a chance to eat, he said to them, "Come with me by yourselves to a quiet place and get some rest" (Mark 6:30-31).

How did you come to realize the importance
of taking care of yourself? What did you do about it?

How did family and friends help you take care of yourself?

What have you learned about taking time for yourself?

What insights do you have to share with other care receivers?

Prayer requests

Answered prayers

Step Nine

Offer Help, But Not Too Much

"Though he stumble, he will not fall, for the Lord upholds him

with his hand" (Psalm 37:24).

Wanda's Story

When Milton first fell ill, I tried to anticipate how to help him before he even asked. I got pretty good at it, too. But I discovered in time that my husband didn't always want my help. Sometimes when I stepped forward to lend a hand, Milton told me gruffly, "I've got it," or, "I can do it myself." His independent streak didn't make much sense to me. Why did he insist on struggling for thirty minutes to put on his shoes when I could do it for him in three? And why would he want to scare me to death by manipulating his power chair on the narrow walkway so he could push the trash barrels to the curb on trash collection day? It would take me no time and little effort to move them myself.

In time, I came to understand Milton's need to do things for himself. I began to trust him when he said, "You don't need to take the trash barrels out tomorrow morning. I put them out tonight so you could sleep in." But I continued to wonder why he usually waited until I wasn't at home to exert his independence. Did my hovering make him anxious? Was he afraid that I would interfere and, in the process, prevent him from discovering ways that *he* could do it? Was he worried that I wouldn't appreciate his effort unless he did it the way I thought it should be done? Did he think I wouldn't understand why he did what he did?

Milton and I both benefited when I encouraged and affirmed his efforts to become more independent of me. How wonderful it was to celebrate his successes with him; to see the control he was able to exert over his own life! I learned to listen when he asked that I move something to a different location so he could more readily get to it. I also learned to be patient as he divided tasks into manageable parts. I learned it wasn't about me but rather about his desire and his need to do things for himself. I learned to support that effort by asking if he needed help rather than assuming he did and by respecting his wishes if he declined my help.

Milt's Story

Wanda says she understands my need for independence, but I'm not sure she really does. Perhaps the thing I dreaded most when I got sick was losing my ability to do things for myself. I detested having to ask for Wanda's help with even the simplest tasks, and I wanted more than anything to regain the abilities I had lost.

I felt a great deal of accomplishment in doing even small things on my own. I realized that I could do things more quickly with Wanda's help, but I didn't care how long it took as long as I did it on my own. Perhaps I would have pushed myself a little harder, but I was concerned about my safety. I didn't do anything rash or heroic because I didn't want to risk having an accident that would delay my recovery. I settled for taking baby steps, but I took them proudly.

One of the goals I set for myself was using the bathroom alone. I saw this goal as a means of regaining some privacy for myself, of which I had precious little. I also understood that achieving this goal would alleviate anxiety for Wanda who, after helping me into public men's rooms, was forced to spend many uncomfortable minutes praying fervently that no one would enter to use the facilities while she waited outside my stall.

When I mastered a skill or accomplished a task, I would pat myself on the back and then look ahead to the next challenge. Even the smallest achievement became for me a personal victory—something I had done on my own. Selfish as it may sound, I wasn't good about sharing my victories with Wanda, even though I knew she would have liked to celebrate my hard won independence with me. My independence represents a lot to me—my dignity, my identity, my hope for a return to life as it was "before," and maybe most important, my role as Wanda's husband. Slowly, but surely, I began to get back on my feet, so to speak. I remain optimistic about the future.

Wanda's Story of Caring Family & Friends

By the time Thanksgiving arrived the first year of Milton's illness, he had little movement in his legs and was confined to his wheelchair. I had contracted pneumonia and certainly did not feel up to preparing for eleven overnight guests and cooking a Thanksgiving feast as well. But, still, we were looking forward to the life, laughter, and love that would soon fill our home. And we were really excited that our two-year-old cousin, Taylor, was coming to visit.

As the holiday approached, I mentioned my concerns about hosting Thanksgiving dinner to my neighbor. Marsha didn't even hesitate before offering to help me with preparations for a traditional holiday feast. "Just make a list," she said, "and I will do the shopping for you." A few days later, while my hairstylist, Janice, was at the house doing my hair, Marsha delivered a mountain of groceries to my kitchen. Dear woman that she is, Janice stayed a while longer to put the food away, and tidied my cupboards in the process.

To help me conserve my energy in the days leading up to Thanksgiving, several friends from church brought in meals for us. This allowed me to concentrate on preparing the foods for our Thanksgiving dinner. As I chopped and whipped and stirred and baked, I thought about the love that permeated my life just as surely as the aroma of turkey and dressing filled my kitchen. In the midst of my preparations, I paused to thank God for his lavish grace poured out on Milton and me through the caring attention of friends who had become to us as family. In the steady parade of people who had come through our front door that week, God had provided all that was needed to make the first Thanksgiving of Milton's illness one of the best Thanksgivings of our lives.

Milt's Story of Caring Family & Friends

I cannot emphasize enough the degree to which my life became focused on coping with unremitting pain. Pain management required enormous concentration and energy on my part, and the moments of reprieve were brief. In the early stages of my condition, I would struggle with some success to focus on something apart from the pain, only to have Wanda interrupt my efforts by asking, "On a scale of one to ten, what is your level of pain?" Her question, although well intended, would immediately return my focus to my pain, which often registered around twelve or thirteen on a ten-point scale. Wanda would then pray aloud, asking God in his grace and mercy to ease my pain.

Our niece, Erin, observed what had become almost a ritual interaction between Wanda and me, and—bless her heart—she recognized what it was doing to me. Drawing Wanda aside, she said, "Aunt Wanda, Uncle Milton probably has found ways to deal with his pain—like losing himself in crossword puzzles, television shows, or jazz music. When you ask how he is feeling, it breaks his concentration and forces him to refocus on the pain he was trying to escape."

Wanda was aghast that her well-meaning attempts to help me manage my pain had had the opposite effect entirely. After Erin's insightful observation, Wanda began to watch more closely, and when she saw that focused look in my eyes, she understood that the best thing she could do for me was to pray silently for God to help me endure my pain.

Although I was already on pain medication, the drugs weren't doing the trick. The quality of our lives changed dramatically when Dr. Kelly McKerahan prescribed a patch to help manage my pain. Perhaps because Kelly was also a friend, he could see what other doctors could not. Kelly could see that I was suffering intense pain in spite of being on medications. But Kelly also recognized the toll my constant battle with pain was taking on Wanda. We both thank God for his insightfulness and for the miracle patch he prescribed. The debilitating pain ended immediately.

Caregiver Tips from Wanda

- Ask what things your care receiver would like to do for himself or herself.

- Work together to identify accommodations to help your care receiver do it independently. Encourage and affirm the efforts of your care receiver to be independent.

- Be flexible. Try not to hover when your care receiver is trying out new things for the first time.

- Celebrate your care receiver's increased independence by reclaiming your own independence.

Care Receiver Tips from Milt

- Share with your caregiver and other family members your need for independence.

- Include your caregiver and other family members in celebrating your hard won accomplishments

- Try to be patient if your caregiver and or family members try to be overly protective.

- Recognize and accept the importance of being safe as you pursue greater and greater levels of independence

- Keep asking your physician about pain management until you are satisfied that he or she is responding.

Respecting Independence

"Cast your cares on the LORD and he will sustain you; he will never let the righteous fall" (Psalm 55:22).

How did you come to realize the importance of not helping too much? How has that affected your care receiver?

What roles have family and friends played in helping care for you and your loved one?

What have you learned about letting go? How has your faith in God affected your actions?

What insights do you have to share with other caregivers?

Prayer requests

Answered prayers

Gaining Independence

"Cast your cares on the LORD and he will sustain you; he will never let the righteous fall" (Psalm 55:22).

How did you come to realize the importance of your independence? How has that affected your caregiver?

What roles have family and friends played in helping care for you and your caregiver?

What have you learned about asserting your independence? How does your faith in God affect your actions?

What insights do you have to share with other care receivers?

Prayer requests

Answered prayers

Step Ten

Deal with Your Anger

"Get rid of all bitterness, rage and anger,

brawling and slander, along with every form of malice.

Be kind and compassionate to one another, forgiving each other,

just as in Christ God forgave you" (Ephesians 4:31-32).

Wanda's Story

At first I refused to acknowledge my anger. "It's nothing, just a minor irritation," I told myself when something upset me. But after a while, I had to admit that I wasn't irritated, I was angry. And more often than I care to admit, my anger was directed at Milton because I felt that he could do more for himself than he was doing.

When Milton could hardly move his legs, I patiently helped him transfer to and from his wheelchair. My patience wore thin, however, as he improved. In spite of the encouragement of his physical therapists and nurse, Milton seemed little inclined to use a walker rather than a wheelchair to cover even short distances. Because I realized how much energy it took him to perform even simple tasks, I continued for a time to lug around his chair for him, growing ever more tired with the effort and increasingly frustrated with my husband with each passing day. Finally, I had had enough. One day as I huffed and puffed trying to get the cumbersome chair out of the car, I decided to speak my mind.

"Milton," I said in no uncertain terms, "I am not lifting this wheelchair out of the car anymore. You can use your walker to go the short distance from the car to physical therapy."

His response? "Well, all right then."

While there would be other times when Milton wouldn't be quite so amenable, that instance taught me a valuable lesson about the importance of addressing "minor irritations" early and of allowing myself to acknowledge my feelings both to my husband and to myself. I came to understand that frequently my anger isn't due to any one thing in particular, but is the result of dealing with the ongoing frustrations of living with chronic illness. I have learned that it helps to consider each situation from Milton's perspective and not only my own. When I do this, I am better able to distinguish when he truly needs my help. I also try to share my feelings as honestly as I can with my husband and to listen to people I love and trust, like my mother, my sister, and my daughter, when they tell me that I'm being stretched too thin and I need to take care of myself. I discovered that exercise helps me feel energized and optimistic, so I joined the physical fitness center in the building where Milton has physical therapy, and I work off my frustrations during his PT appointments. I know that my anger is not healthy for me or for my husband, and so I pray for God's help in overcoming it even while rejoicing in the knowledge that family and friends are faithfully praying for us as well.

Milt's Story

"Those whom the gods would destroy, they first make angry" (Seneca). This ancient quote was a favorite of my mother's, and I agree with the wisdom it imparts. Anger is a destructive force. Medical studies show that anger can be harmful to our health, and the Bible also speaks of the power of anger to destroy relationships and lives.

I've discovered that the old strategy of counting to ten helps diffuse my anger in most situations. In fact, I seldom get beyond number nine. On the rare occasions I do get angry, I turn to prayer and reflection to help quiet my temper. I try not to let small things upset me, and I have found that praying for discernment helps me keep things in proper perspective. It's amazing how minor even my most major frustrations seem after a few minutes in conversation with the Lord.

As my condition deteriorated, I found comfort and strength in the witness of St. Paul, who suffered mightily from an affliction described only as "a thorn in [his] flesh" (2 Corinthians 12:7). Like Paul, I have accepted my condition, and I try to deal with it as positively as I can, knowing that God has blessed me by keeping me from further harm during the course of my illness. I continue to ask God to allow me to be a blessing to others by my example and by my witness.

Wanda finds it hard to believe that I feel it has been important for me to experience the pain, physical limitations, and dependency on others imposed by my illness. As one who had known excellent health for much of my life, embracing my illness has allowed me to better understand and relate to others who live with chronic illness and acute pain. While growing up, whenever I balked at new experiences, my mother was famous for saying, "One day you will understand better." My journey through illness has certainly shown that to be true.

Wanda's Story of Caring Family & Friends

Milton was engaged in something—I don't remember what—when I called him to come to the table because dinner was nearly ready. "Call me again when dinner is on the table," he called back to me. In retrospect, I can see that my response to Milton's comment was over-the-top, but I sure didn't see it that way then. I was livid that he seemed to think his time was too important to waste sitting at the table while I rushed about attending to last-minute meal preparations. Just who did he think he was anyway?

While I don't remember exactly what I said to my husband, I do know that I let go with a torrent of pent-up frustration and hurt directed straight at him. Unfortunately, my response to Milton's comment was poorly timed as both my mother and sister were visiting and heard my tirade. My sister, Pat, took me aside later to share their concern. "Wanda, I can only imagine the stress you are under and only you could pull all of this off—caring for Milton, being a great hostess, and keeping your home so inviting. But, honey, it seems to be taking its toll. Your anger is beginning to overshadow the wonderful things we all love about you." Pat went on to suggest that I consider talking with a professional counselor about what was going on in our lives and the strain Milton's illness was placing on me.

I knew Pat was right. I didn't like being angry and it was obvious that my anger wasn't doing Milton or me any good. To this day, I am eternally grateful that Pat dared to speak up out of love and concern for me and for Milton. Without her intervention, I don't know that I would have recognized that I needed help. Shortly after that, I began seeing a professional counselor. Over the next weeks and months I learned much about myself, and I gained skills that are helpful in avoiding unnecessary conflict and in defusing stressful situations before they have a chance to escalate. As time passed and new situations and challenges arose, I continued to check in periodically with my counselor and to learn from her insights.

Milt's Story of Caring Family & Friends

Christmas came early to our house in a gift delivered by a brother in Christ from my Monday Night Football group. Cecil stopped by on a hot day in July to add carpeting to the wheelchair ramps he and another brother named Howard had built a few days earlier. When the job took less time than anticipated, Cecil gallantly asked Wanda if there was something more he could do to help. "How about the garage?" he asked, alluding to the chaos of plaster, wood, and other debris that still hadn't been cleaned up after my infamous driving incident.

The garage had been worrying Wanda for some time, but lacking the physical and emotional stamina to tackle the mess, she had chosen not to deal with it until later. Sensing that "later" had arrived earlier than expected, Wanda clasped her hands in sheer joy and thanksgiving, and eagerly responded, "That would be great." Thanks to Cecil, the garage was soon restored to order, although major repair work on the guest bath wall and laundry room door still needed to be accomplished.

This was the first of many times that Cecil provided much appreciated practical assistance that made life easier for us. On another occasion he installed an outside light that helped both Wanda and me feel safer. After I fell in the bathroom, cracking the toilet tank in the process, Cecil put in a new toilet. He also spent part of a day repairing a hole in the laundry room wall that I had made when I slammed the door into the wall while speeding up the ramp in my power chair. But Cecil wasn't only a heaven-sent handyman. He was God's answer to the frustration I was feeling because I could no longer take care of things around the house. Cecil helped relieve some of my concern for Wanda, whose plate was already too full even without the added responsibility of dealing with household chores. Thank the Lord for Christmas celebrated early on hot days in mid-summer!

Caregiver Tips from Wanda

- Identify situations that cause anger and change those you can change. Decide how you will respond to those you cannot change.

- Cut some slack for yourself and the person with whom you are angry.

- Lovingly share your feelings with the person with whom you are angry. Try to resolve the issues as soon as possible so you are not taking your anger to bed with you.

- Ask forgiveness from the one/ones who are the recipients of your anger. Forgive as you would want to be forgiven.

- Find a close family member or friend with whom you can talk.

- Know when it is time to seek professional help and do so.

- Be open to sharing with others how counseling has helped you so it may be less intimidating for them should they need to seek professional help.

- Pray.

Care Receiver Tips from Milt

- Count to ten before reacting.

- Try to keep things in perspective.

- Turn to the Bible for some great role models.

- Focus on being a role model and a blessing to others.

Dealing with Anger

"The LORD is gracious and compassionate, slow to anger and rich in love" (Psalm 145:8).

Tell about a time when you acknowledged
and dealt with your anger.

Who among your family and friends provided support
for you during this time?

What lessons did you learn?

What insights do you have to share with other caregivers?

Prayer requests

Answered prayers

Dealing with Anger

"The LORD is gracious and compassionate, slow to anger and rich in love" (Psalm 145:8).

Tell about a time when you acknowledged and dealt with your anger.

Who among your family and friends provided support for you during this time?

What lessons did you learn?

What insights do you have to share
with other care receivers?

Prayer requests

Answered prayers

Step Eleven

Let Go of Your Guilt

"If we confess our sins, he is faithful and just

and will forgive us our sins and purify us

from all unrighteousness" (1 John 1:9).

Wanda's Story

After the onset of Milton's illness, I found myself on many occasions asking, "Why?" Why did Milton go on that mission trip to Mexico? Why didn't he go to the doctor sooner? Why did my husband think that it was necessary to continue driving even when it put him and others at risk? Why was Milton so insistent about trying to do things on his own? These questions were often followed by a litany of blame. It's Milton's fault that we can't fly to Seattle to spend Christmas with family like we always have. It's his fault we have to make financial accommodations to cover large medical expenses. It's his fault that our house looks more like a therapy center than a home.

On the one hand, I was sincerely thankful for our many blessings, which included great insurance coverage, helpful friends and family, and an understanding employer who allowed Milton to continue working from home, as he was able. On the other hand, I suffered mightily from "woe is me" syndrome. How often I protested, albeit silently so only God could hear, that this wasn't how I had planned to live my life! Then I would be overcome with guilt and I would wonder, "What kind of person am I? What would others think of me if they knew how I really felt?" It was very difficult knowing that, while others might not perceive my selfishness, God was well aware of my unChrist-like attitude.

In time the guilt and blame I carried in my heart began to affect me physically. I suffered from a variety of ailments as well as from an overwhelming sense of sadness. When these burdens finally grew too heavy to bear, I called out to God to forgive me. And he did! In spite of everything, I truly felt as if I had been given a fresh start, as if God had wiped clean the white board on which I had recorded all of my horrible thoughts. Thank you, Lord!

Milt's Story

I decided early in my illness that if I was going to survive, I would not be able to spend precious time and energy on the destructive forces of guilt and blame. I made a conscious decision to focus whatever resources I had on my recovery. I worked hard to keep a positive attitude and to move forward as quickly as possible. Maybe it's a male thing. Men like to travel light. We hate being encumbered with a lot of baggage. I guess I just wasn't willing to carry the added weight of guilt and blame on my journey through illness.

From the time Wanda and I were newlyweds, we have been intentional about living according to scripture's admonishment, "Do not let the sun go down while you are still angry." This passage from Ephesians 4:26 has kept us from going to bed angry on many occasions over the course of close to forty years of marriage. In these last years, I've found that saying, "I'm sorry," helps relieve the guilt I easily could feel for the burdens my illness has placed upon Wanda. I've also turned to another Bible passage to help me "lose the guilt" that threatens to weigh me down and make it even harder for me to stand. Psalm 103:12 says, "As far as the east is from the west, so far has [God] removed our transgressions from us." On especially difficult days, when I'm reminded all too often of my own unChrist-like, this passage reassures me of the power and presence of forgiveness in my life—forgiveness that restores relationships and keeps us traveling light.

Wanda's Story of Caring Family & Friends

I remember watching our usually exuberant grandson, Jay, walk dejectedly out of school one afternoon. I learned soon enough that Jay had gotten into a little trouble in class and was not looking forward to telling me or Opa about it. "But are you sorry?" I asked after he told me what had happened.

"Oh, yes, Oma," he assured me.

"And will you try really hard not to do it again?" I continued.

"I promise, Oma," he added with eyes downcast.

"Then you are forgiven. God has forgiven you, I forgive you, and I can assure you that Opa will forgive you," I proclaimed joyfully.

"Really, Oma?" he asked, unable to believe his good fortune.

"Really!" I replied emphatically, and with that Jay became his usual happy self.

My conversation with Jay was fresh in my mind as I struggled to forgive myself for feeling frustrated and even angry about the demands of Milton's care. It seemed that while I could tell my grandson with absolute conviction that he could trust in God's forgiveness, I hadn't quite claimed that forgiveness for myself. In other words, I wasn't practicing what I preached.

When we forgive someone—even ourselves—we give up control. Could it be that, because I already had lost so much control over my life, I wasn't willing to relinquish anything more—even the wrongs I had committed—to God? I thought back to my conversation with Jay, and I remembered how he had played with such abandon that evening. He had eaten heartily at dinner and slept peacefully through the night because, in the blessed assurance of God's forgiveness, Jay had forgiven himself the wrong he had committed.

I learned an important, life-changing lesson that day from my grandson who even then was wise beyond his years. "And a little child will lead them" (Isaiah 11:6).

Milt's Story of Caring Family & Friends

Wanda and I have a grandson, Jay, who lives in Germany. Prior to the onset of my illness, Jay's visits to our home included hours of playing together in our pool. Jay loves to swim, and so I wondered how our relationship would change now that horseplay in the pool was no longer possible.

I soon discovered that Jay was as content watching basketball together on television as he had been swimming with me in the pool. While I was very happy for our easy rapport, I found myself wondering how this twelve-year-old boy could be so comfortable around me with all my physical limitations. We hadn't talked about my illness, but Jay seemed to understand my situation nevertheless. Over the course of Jay's visit, I gradually came to realize that I had Jay's other grandfather, Opa Willy, to thank for my grandson's understanding.

Wanda and I had visited Germany on several occasions and been guests of Willy and his wife, Hilde, so I knew, of course, that Willy was confined to a wheelchair. But I hadn't really given much thought to this fact, nor to how Jay related to his other grandfather, until the onset of my own illness. Now I realized that Jay's experience growing up with Opa Willy was responsible for his immediate comfort with me and my changed situation and his uncanny ability to anticipate and meet my needs. What a gift Willy and Hilde gave me by instilling in Jay such wonderful, caring attributes! Thanks to them, Jay understood that my physical limitations had no bearing whatsoever on my love for him.

Jay's visit with us came to an end far too soon. We arrived at the airport early, after a night of very little sleep, and while Jay and Wanda waited in line to take care of last-minute flight arrangements, I found a spot by a sunny window to park my wheelchair. Evidently I dozed off because the next thing I remember is Jay gently shaking me awake so he and I could spend a few more precious minutes together before he returned to Germany. As we sat talking, I thought about how concerned I had been that my illness would get in the way of my relationship with my grandson. How wrong I had been! Because of my illness, I experienced first-hand the rich, unconditional love of a grandson for a grandfather. God bless you, Jay, and thank you, Opa Willy.

Tips from the Caregiver & the Care Receiver

Caregiver tips from Wanda

- Pray.

- Acknowledge your guilt and identify its source.

- Try to address the issues you can address.

- Find a trustworthy and compassionate family member or friend with whom to talk.

- Talk with the care receiver for whom you are caring, if it seems appropriate.

- Ask for their forgiveness if it is needed.

- Most important of all, *forgive yourself.*

Care Receiver Tips from Milt

- Recognize that guilt is not healthy for you or for those around you.

- Admit when you are wrong and say you are sorry.

- If your mistake is a big one, be ready to ask forgiveness; then forgive yourself.

- Communicate with your caregiver how you are really feeling.

- Try to resolve misunderstandings as soon as possible.

Letting Go of Guilt

"As far as the east is from the west, so far has he removed our transgressions from us" *(Psalm 103:12).*

Describe a time in which you acknowledged
and dealt with your guilt.

What family members or friends provided support
for you as you struggled with guilt?

What lessons have you learned about guilt and its affect
on you? What have you learned about God's love and
compassion?

What insights do you have to share with other caregivers?

Prayer requests

Answered prayer

Letting Go of Guilt

"As far as the east is from the west, so far has he removed our transgressions from us" (Psalm 103:12).

Describe a time in which you acknowledged
and dealt with your guilt.

What family members or friends provided support
for you as you struggled with guilt?

What lessons have you learned about guilt and its affect
on you? What have you learned about God's love and
compassion?

What insights do you have to share with other care receivers?

Prayer requests

Answered prayer

Step Twelve

Affirm Yourself and Count Your Blessings

"But the fruit of the Spirit is love, joy, peace, patience,

kindness, goodness, faithfulness, gentleness and self-control"

(Galatians 5:22-23a).

Wanda's Story

When Milton first became ill, I would spend time at the end of each day lamenting all the things I hadn't gotten done that day. Even as others affirmed the fine job I was doing as Milton's caregiver, I seemed unable to see beyond my long list of unaccomplished tasks.

One Sunday, our niece, Erin, and her husband, Patrick, came to check up on us. As Erin walked through the house, she commented on the many accommodations we had made in our home to provide for Milton's needs and our sense of wellbeing. When the tour ended, I asked, "When you leave today, will you immediately call your mother and grandmother to report on how we are doing?"

"Yes, Aunt Wanda," Erin confirmed, "You know that the family is anxiously waiting for my call."

Curious, I asked, "And what will you tell them?"

Without thinking twice, Erin assured me, "I will tell them how well you and Uncle Milton are doing and what a great adjustment you both have made. You are doing a fantastic job, Aunt Wanda."

Erin's assessment of our situation and her affirmation of me as a caregiver were exactly what I needed. From that day on, rather than bemoaning what I hadn't gotten done, I began acknowledging at the end of each day all that I had accomplished. I gave thanks for the strength God provided me to do the things I needed to do and for the people God sent to help me. I also gave thanks for my husband, whose positive and faithful spirit as care receiver made my role as caregiver ever so much easier. What a difference it made when I began to celebrate these victories! I had always "counted my blessings" before I went to bed, but now I really began to savor the joy of knowing God's continued faithfulness in the activities of each day. I went to bed feeling love, joy, peace, patience, and kindness toward Milton *and* myself, and I awoke to face each new day with anticipation and hope. I felt good about myself and believed that God had, indeed, blessed me with the gifts needed to be my husband's caregiver.

Milt's Story

I have always believed I would walk again some day, and from the beginning I set benchmarks to help me achieve that goal. One of the first goals was to be able to transfer from the recliner in our great room to my wheelchair. That goal was especially important to me because it meant Wanda no longer would have to bear a good deal of my weight during the transfer. Meeting this goal was also a big step in my independence. Wanda actually could go to a meeting or get her hair done, knowing that I wasn't going to be confined to my recliner until she returned.

I also set goals for dressing myself. On Sunday mornings Wanda would have to get up extra early to help me dress before she left for church to set up for the 8:00 service. Wanda is an organist, and she appreciates having some quiet time before the service to get ready. I really felt good when I reached my goal and Wanda no longer had to help me get dressed and put on my compression hose. It felt good because while I was increasing my level of independence, I was decreasing my level of dependence on Wanda. I wanted her to have her own life. I didn't want her to have to give up the things she enjoyed doing just because I needed so much of her help.

Step Twelve says to "affirm yourself." I would rather use the words, "feel good about yourself." After reaching each goal, I would have a little celebration in my head, quickly followed by giving thanks to God. I've never taken for granted the many ways God has blessed me and continues to bless me.

Wanda's Story of Caring Family & Friends

I started out calling her Dr. Mary, this wonderful woman who just happened to be the same age as my mother. When we first met, Dr. Mary Howell was seventy-eight years old and still maintaining a medical practice. How did she do it? I think her positive attitude contributed a lot. One of Dr. Mary's favorite sayings was, "Do your best and let God do the rest." I took Dr. Mary's sage advice to heart and liberally applied it as I faced and met the new challenges in my role as a caregiver.

Over the years, our relationship developed into something more than doctor/patient. We became dear friends. While I deeply appreciated Dr. Mary's healing touch, it was the love and encouragement she showed me that made me love her. It just seemed natural one day that I call her, Mother Mary. "Is that all right?" I asked anxiously.

"Of course," she replied. "I can be your California Mama."

I laughed. What other kind of response would I expect from my Mother Mary, ninety-one and still going strong?

I welcomed Dorene with open arms as she tearfully recounted a personal issue facing her. Over the following weeks, then months, I was ready with a listening ear. One day, I realized that not only was Dorene receiving my support, she was providing support to me as well. Eventually she began inviting me out to be with other women for much needed fun and fellowship. She also prayed daily for my daughter, Shelly, saying she really appreciated how Shelly was willing to share her mom with her.

I don't know whether to call Dorene an affirming friend or a role model. How did she manage everything in her life? She was mother to five children between the ages of four and fifteen and she worked with me in women's ministry at our church. Yet she found the time to help a friend who tragically lost her husband, organizing a meal to feed the 400 to 500 guests at the memorial service. How did she maintain such a positive attitude? My guess is that as she blessed others, she was blessed in return.

Milt's Story of Caring Family & Friends

Keala is Wanda's Hawaiian sister. They first became friends when they were elected to our church's women's regional board of directors. Wanda offered to pick up Keala from the airport whenever she flew in for board meetings, and it seemed natural that Keala would spend a night or two with Wanda and me. Keala soon became friends with my Friday morning Bible study group that met in our home, and when she was in town, she would bring gifts for them. After I became ill, we wondered if Keala would still feel comfortable staying with us, since our home resembled a medical device store. There was no reason to worry. Upon her arrival, Keala checked in on me. She was her usual positive, friendly self, laughing and making jokes. "Milt, it is amazing all the things you can do on your own," Keala observed. Those simple words of encouragement meant so much! She recognized how hard I was working to regain my independence.

And Keala had more love and encouragement to share. When she heard that Cowboy, one of my Bible study members, could no longer attend because of a serious condition he was battling, Keala decided to bring hula dolls the next time she came to town. After I told the guys, they eagerly anticipated Keala's next visit and her promised gifts. Did I mention that Keala was as beautiful on the outside as she was on the inside? Arrangements were made to deliver Cowboy's gift to him. The guys noticed that Cowboy's hula doll was a larger version of theirs. "Hmmm," they thought but quickly agreed it was all right since it was for Cowboy. As we concluded our Bible study, the phone rang. It was Cowboy wondering what was taking us so long to get his hula doll to him. Who knew a hula doll could mean so much! It must have been the love and care that Keala packed with each doll that made it special.

Love, I've decided, has got to be the best affirmation of all. I recommend a liberal dose. It is great for keeping up your spirits. I found it is much easier for me to affirm myself when others around me are so affirming.

Caregiver Tips from Wanda

- Think about the ways God has gifted you for this particular role.

- Focus on what you have done right instead of on what has gone wrong or hasn't been done.

- Decide to let anyone who is critical own his or her own feelings. Resist explaining your actions or trying to win the approval of others.

- Encourage and support a positive environment by affirming the positive efforts of your care receiver as well as others who come to help.

- Remember to do things that help you feel good about yourself and that give you additional opportunities to be affirmed by others.

Care Receiver Tips from Milt

- Try to be calm in times of stress.

- Remember that patience is a virtue.

- Enjoy the simple things of life.

- Count your blessings.

Counting Your Blessings

"That everyone may eat and drink, and find satisfaction in all his toil—this is the gift of God" (Ecclesiastes 3:13).

When was the last time you gave yourself a pat on the back for a job well done?

Who among your family and friends do you count as special blessings? How has God worked through them to help you?

What lessons have you learned about God's blessings?

What insights do you have to share with other caregivers?

Prayer requests

Answered prayers

Counting Your Blessings

"That everyone may eat and drink, and find satisfaction in all his toil—this is the gift of God" (Ecclesiastes 3:13).

When was the last time you gave yourself a pat on the back for a job well done?

Who among your family and friends do you count as special blessings? How has God worked through them to help you?

What lessons have you learned about God's blessings?

What insights do you have to share with other care receivers?

Prayer requests

Answered prayers

Epilogue

Our Journey Continues . . .

Dear Readers,

Milton and I are now approaching our third year of treatment. We have come a long way! Milton continues to receive his IVIg treatment two times a week, and, as a result, the nerve linings in his legs have been growing back, albeit very slowly. However, he is now able to walk—yes, walk with the aid of a walker—for a whole block before he has to sit down and rest! We are delighted and so grateful to God. Milton also took himself off all his pain medications and rejoices that his thinking is no longer foggy.

The crowning glory for me occurred just a few weeks ago when Milton informed me on our way home from church that he wanted to stop in and pray for our next-door neighbor who has cancer. I parked the car and got Milton's walker out for him. Ever so carefully, he walked down our driveway over to our neighbor's driveway. Since they don't have ramps, he had to lift his walker up over the door's threshold. He spent a few minutes talking with our neighbor and then prayed for him, before starting the long journey back home. He truly was magnificent!

We are also pleased to report that Milton has begun traveling to conferences, a requirement of his job. I was scared for him, but God has provided a supportive employer, ingenious airplane baggage handlers to load and unload his heavy power chair, wonderful hotel staff, and an absolutely blessed van driver to get him to and from his destination. Milton is so pleased with himself. It is another step in his commitment to regain all of his former independence.

My life is not nearly so exciting as Milton's, but I rejoice in his independence, which allows me to reclaim mine. I truly love my life of working in our church, inspirational speaking as I tell our story—at least my half of it—and the mentoring I am starting to do with people who are struggling as caregivers. God is truly good. We give him all the praise and glory. Please pray for us. And so we come to the last "step" in this book—the Thirteenth Step that sums up it all—faith. Looking ahead, we are calling on an extra measure of faith in our lives. There is much more to accomplish and, we hope, many more joys to celebrate. It brings us strength to know that God will be with us through it all. At the same time, we would like to share some of that faith with you—faith in God to be with you, to show you the way, to provide wonderful family, friends, and health professionals who can help you in your journey, to bless you and keep you. The prophet Jeremiah said it best, "'For I know the plans I have for you,' declares the LORD, 'plans to prosper you and not to harm you, plans to give you hope and a future. Then you will call upon me and come and pray to me, and I will listen to you'" (Jeremiah 29:11-12).

Milton and I pray that the reading of this book and the development of your own story of journeying together through illness will mean as much to you as writing about our journey has meant to us.

May God bless you and keep you in his loving care.

—Wanda and Milt Bledsoe